JIM PEYTON'S

THE VERY BEST OF

TEX-MEX COOKING

PLUS TEXAS BARBEQUE AND

TEXAS CHILE

JIM PEYTON'S
THE VERY BEST OF
TEX-MEX
COOKING

PLUS TEXAS BARBECUE AND
TEXAS CHILE

Maverick Publishing Company / *San Antonio*

ALSO BY JIM PEYTON

El Norte: The Cuisine of Northern Mexico

La cocina de la frontera: Mexican-American Cooking from the Southwest

Jim Peyton's New Cooking from Old Mexico

Copyright © 2005 by James W. Peyton

MAVERICK PUBLISHING COMPANY
P.O. Box 6355, San Antonio, Texas 78209

Library of Congress Cataloging-in-Publication Data
Peyton, James W.
Jim Peyton's the very best of Tex-Mex cooking plus Texas barbecue and
Texas chile / James W. Peyton.
p. cm.
Includes index.
ISBN 1-893271-33-1 (alk. paper)
1. Cookery, American–Southwestern style.
2. Mexican American cookery.
I. Title: Very best of Tex-Mex cooking plus Texas barbecue and Texas chile.
II. Title.
TX715.2.S69P486 2004
641.5979–dc22   2004018878

Drawings by Andrea Peyton
Book and cover design by Barbara Whitehead

10 9 8 7 6 5 4 3 2

CONTENTS

It was never hard to find Mexican food in San Antonio, where Tex-Mex food first got established in the United States. Here chili con carne was served to passersby on Military Plaza in the 1880s.

PREFACE

The "Very Best of Tex-Mex Cooking" means the very best of what I have determined to be the dishes people order most often in their favorite Tex-Mex restaurants.

These recipes have developed organically as Texas regional cooking over many years of trial and error by thousands of remarkable cooks. They have become enormously popular not just in Texas but nationwide, and, increasingly, worldwide.

The problem is that although Tex-Mex in the hands of accomplished cooks can reach heights of culinary excellence, too often it falls far short of that mark, leading some to a derogatory view of the cuisine. Too many restaurants provide the basic flavor but not the highest quality of Tex-Mex, and do not offer the culinary sophistication of Tex-Mex at its best. Too many cookbooks perpetuate this mediocrity by including as many recipes as possible, without regard for quality. They may reflect the actual spectrum of Tex-Mex food out there, but I don't care what you pour Velveeta cheese over, it doesn't taste that good.

Many people indeed grew up on Tex-Mex food made with cheese substitutes and other low-quality items, which may be edible and nostalgic for them. But I think they would agree with those coming from elsewhere that the more refined ingredients used by the genre's best cooks make better Tex-Mex.

Here are the recipes for that cooking.

Since some cooks desire in-depth information about what they will be making, the history, techniques and secrets for each dish are thoroughly covered in the recipe introductions. For cooks primarily interested in actual preparation, each introduction is followed by recipes with simple, concise instructions for the very best!

With the success of their open-air food stands, some vendors began serving in their homes, as at this 1890s "fonda" in San Antonio, as Tex-Mex restaurants evolved.

INTRODUCTION

For Texas to win independence from Mexico, become a republic and carve vast ranching and petroleum empires from a hostile environment required independent and self-assertive citizens. Today's Texans combine those traits with what outsiders sometimes characterize as an unseemly passion for their accomplishments and traditions.

Make no mistake, Tex-Mex, Texas barbecue and Texas chile are traditions that can quickly turn simmering self-assertiveness into contentiousness. To this day controversies rage throughout South Texas over who made the first nacho or margarita, whether or not barbecued brisket should have a final roasting in foil and whether beans should be served with chile or on the side. It therefore seems probable that anyone attempting to write about something so near and dear to a Texan's heart would do so with trepidation. However, drawing on our native self confidence and many years experience in the subject, we never hesitated!

The cooking of Mexico's interior, as we know it today, began in the sixteenth century with the fusion of Spanish and Indian cooking. Tex-Mex was begun by Mexicans working on ranches in South Texas, and expanded later by others who immigrated in the early twentieth century to avoid the anarchy of the Mexican Revolution.

Coming largely from the northern Mexican states of Coahuila, Nuevo Leon and Tamaulipas, the immigrants adapted their recipes to accommodate ingredients and cooking equipment found north of the border to produce what is now called Tex-Mex. Most significant were the plentiful supplies of beef and ovens, items that were scarce in Mexico.

Dining Room of the Mitla Mexican Restaurant,
219 Losoya Street :: San Antonio, Texas

Mexican food went mainstream in San Antonio following the arrival of large numbers of refugees from the Mexican Revolution of 1910. The Mitla Mexican Restaurant welcomed diners with a pot of cactus at the entrance, featured Mexican drawings on the walls and replicated patterns from the ruins of Mitla in southern Mexico in a frieze near the ceiling.

While Mexican cooking has always been a strong element of South Texas ranch cooking, prior to World War II Mexicans were often separated from the Anglo majority in urban areas. However, the war effort brought the groups closer together as many Mexican-Americans moved to cities to work in factories. Many started restaurants featuring their Tex-Mex cooking. Once Anglos sampled this nearly habit-forming cuisine they were hooked. A greater understanding of Mexican-Americans and the opportunity to sample their cooking began the process by which Tex-Mex became part of the Texas and national cuisines.

While most authentic Tex-Mex cooking is still found in Texas, particularly in South Texas, where it began, increasingly there are restaurants serving Tex-Mex in many other states and on other continents.

One frequent question is whether or not Tex-Mex is really Mexican. The answer is an emphatic YES. Tex-Mex is a legitimate, regional style of Mexican cooking, a Mexican-American cousin rather than brother or sister, but nevertheless, as we say in Texas, blood kin.

x

Menu

REGULAR SUPPER, 35c
Consists of

Tamales	Frijoles
Chile con Carne	Tortillas de Maiz
Enchilada	Sopa de Arroz

Café

SPECIAL SUPPER, 60c

Chile con Queso

Chile con Carne	Tamales	Sopa de Arroz
Frijoles	Enchiladas	Chile Relleno
Piña		Café

SPECIAL SUPPER, $1.00

Chile con Queso
Ensalada de Aguacate

Chile con Carne		Sopa de Arroz
	Frijoles	Tamales
Taco		Chile Relleno
	Enchilada	
Piña		Dulce
Café	Té	Chocolate

SHORT ORDERS

Chile con Carne	.15	Chiles Rellenos	.20
Frijoles	.10	Mole Poblano	
Frijoles con Tortillas	.15	Pollo con Arroz	
Sopa de Arroz	.10	Chile con Queso	.20
Sopa de Arroz con		Pollo con Calabaza	
Tortillas	.15	Guajolote	
Tamales	.15	Albondigas de Arroz	
Tamales con Salsa	.20	Fritoque	.25
Enchiladas	.20	Pescado	
Enchiladas con Huevos	30	Ensalada de Aguacate	
Huevos con Salsa	.20	Té	.05
Huevos Rancheros	.20	Leche	.05
Tácos	.20	Café	.05
Tortillas de Maiz	.05	Chocolate	.10
Chalupas	.20		

San Antonio's Original Mexican Restaurant in the 1930s brought a touch of Spanish Colonial Revival architecture to its exterior. Indoors it offered diners Tex-Mex plates for 35 cents, 60 cents or a dollar.

XI

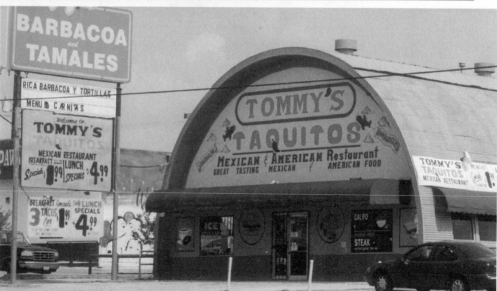

Tex-Mex food, spread throughout the nation and even the world, is still ubiquitous in its San Antonio home in places from the relatively upscale Pico de Gallo to neighborhood spots like Tommy's Taquitos.

That does not mean there are not significant differences between Tex-Mex and interior Mexican cooking, just as there are differences between the cooking of different regions within Mexico. The distinctive gravy-style enchilada sauces and the use of cheddar cheese and ground beef—ubiquitous in Tex-Mex cooking— are rarely encountered south of the border. Also, Tex-Mex relies to a very large extent on *antojitos mexicanos*—the corn- and tortilla-based specialties such as enchiladas, tamales and tacos that are only one aspect of south-of-the-border cooking. The Tex-Mex tradition of a combination plate, covered in red chile sauce and melted cheese, is also unique to this side of the border.

Another frequent query involves differences between Tex-Mex and other styles of Mexican-American cooking found in such places as Arizona and New Mexico—and far West Texas, where the Mexican food often resembles that of New Mexico more than Tex-Mex.

One important difference from those places is that Tex-Mex cooking uses much more beef and cumin, especially in its all-important enchilada sauces. Also, Tex-Mex includes several important dishes, including carne guisada and puffy tacos, that are almost never found in other styles.

On the other hand, some dishes, such as burritos and chimichangas, the mainstays of Arizona/Sonora style cooking, and sopaipillas, found throughout New Mexico, are almost never served in Tex-Mex restaurants, or, for that matter, in south Texas homes. Another significant difference is that Tex-Mex flour tortillas are often thicker than those of other styles.

People from other parts of the country are often concerned that Tex-Mex ingredients will be difficult to find. Fortunately, that is rarely a problem. Tex-Mex is a simple cuisine, with relatively few ingredients, most readily available in even small grocery stores. Because of the large Hispanic population in the southwestern United States, almost any supermarket will stock all items called for in these recipes. In other parts of the country where a few such items as ancho chiles or chile powder made with ancho chiles may be harder to find, they can be located in specialty groceries or, often more easily, with a telephone call to one of the sources listed in the appendix.

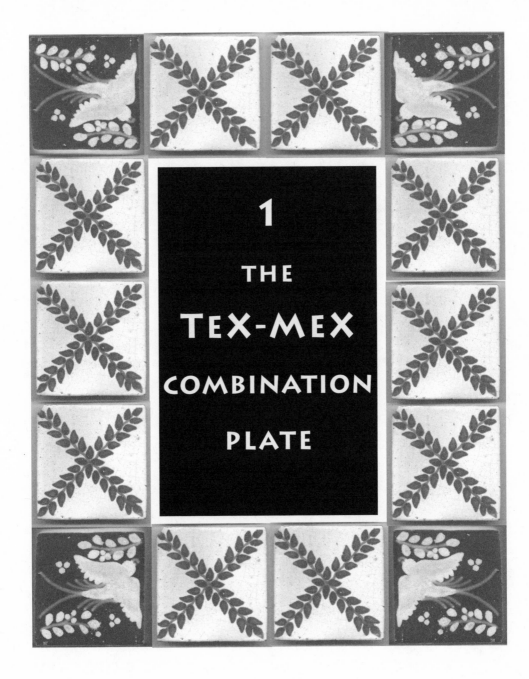

1

THE
TEX-MEX
COMBINATION
PLATE

THE
TEX-MEX
COMBINATION PLATE

Almost any owner of a Tex-Mex restaurant will tell you that the establishment's most popular items are their combination plates. These dishes echo the simple, casual meals served in homes and almost always include Mexican-style rice and refried beans plus two or more other items, such as enchiladas, tacos, tostadas, *quesadillas* or *flautas.*

Families often serve these foods home-style, on separate platters from which diners help themselves. In restaurants they are combined on a single plate and given different names, such as The Tex-Mex Combo, or The #1 Combination Plate, depending on what is included. A few restaurants have responded to customers' requests to substitute items on their listed combination plates by simply listing all the items, then noting how many of them may be included with rice, beans, salsa and tortillas at various prices.

In that spirit, this book has been organized to place all items that relate to the most popular combination plates in this first section. Taken together the recipes will allow you to craft your own favorite combinations.

For example, the most typical combination plate is one that features a cheese enchilada, Tex-Mex style tamale, a crisp taco filled with *picadillo,* Mexican rice, refried beans and a garnish of shredded lettuce. All are arranged on one plate, and the enchilada and tamale are covered with a sizzling hot red chile sauce and shredded cheese. The meal is preceded by a basket of warm, crisp tortilla chips, a bowl or two of salsa, perhaps a platter of *nachos,* and is accompanied by steaming corn and/or flour tortillas. While most combination plates feature at least one enchilada with red chile sauce, some do not, and this is where you exercise your preferences, mixing and matching to create your own favorite.

APPETIZERS AND SALSAS

I n virtually all Tex-Mex restaurants, customers are given a free basket of tortilla chips and salsa and many order an additional appetizer, such as guacamole or nachos. Therefore, we begin our presentation of the Tex-Mex combination plate recipes with those items.

TOTOPOS
(Tortilla Chips)

T he chips-and-salsa appetizer is one of the few examples, in addition to the margarita, of Mexican food moving south. Until a few years ago not many south-of-the-border restaurants served a complimentary basket of crispy, golden-brown tortilla chips to newly seated customers. That has changed and this tasty item has become almost *de rigueur* even in exclusive Mexico City establishments. The movement probably began when border town restaurants discovered that their gringo customers were disappointed when they didn't receive the anticipated welcome, and gradually, the custom spread deep into the interior. Restaurateurs then discovered it was not just *norte americanos* who appreciate this now-universal appetizer.

Like so many other Mexican foods, preparation of chips has unexpected subtleties. First, they are at their lightest and best when made with the thin, dry American-style corn tortillas. However, while the razor-thin variety produces the crispest, most delicate texture, medium-thick tortillas, if quite dry, will expand, almost explode, when fried at the right temperature, creating a chip with two light, crispy sides.

Which brings us to another important item: the frying temperature. Too low a heat will ensure a soggy result, too much heat an unpleasant, burned flavor and cracker-like texture. The best temperature is 345 to 355 degrees.

The frying medium is also important as each produces a different flavor. Most restaurants use commercial products not available in grocery stores, which are designed to be used over and over without imparting an off taste. Lard makes hands down the most flavorful chips, but most home cooks shy away from it. They are wise to do so, as most super market lard is of poor quality and made with hydrogenated fats. One compromise is to add a small amount of lard or bacon to other fats, such as corn, peanut, canola, soy or just plain vegetable oil. Again, remember that each one will produce a different flavor, so I suggest you experiment.

My favorite combination is to add 1/2 tablespoon lard or 1/3 large piece bacon to each cup of corn oil. If using bacon, remember to remove the pieces well before they burn.

To fry the chips, you can use an electric deep fryer or a large pot with a deep fry thermometer. Bear in mind that thermostats on deep fryers made for home use are often inaccurate, so it is a good idea to use another thermometer at least until you have learned how yours is calibrated. The handiest ones are those that clip to the side of the fryer or pot.

If you use a regular pot, select one that is fairly wide and, for safety, deep enough so that when cold the oil comes to no more than halfway to the top. Five cups of oil will allow you to fry chips made from 4 tortillas at one time.

Totopos

Oil for deep frying
1/2 tablespoon lard or 1/3 large piece bacon per cup of oil
    (optional)
1 dozen corn tortillas

Heat the oil to 350 degrees. If you are using bacon, put it in when the oil is cold and remove it just as it turns golden brown. While the oil is heating, arrange the tortillas on a cutting board in a stack, one on top of the other.

Cut through the center of the circle to make 2 half-circles. Next, cut each half-circle into 2 equal-sized pieces This will leave you with 48 triangle-shaped pieces. In three batches, place the tortilla pieces in the hot oil and—even if you are using a sub-mersible fryer basket—press them into the oil with a slotted spoon or spatula.

The chips will be done when the bubbles in the oil subside and the chips are just beginning to turn golden. After they are removed they will continue to cook and become slightly darker.

Remove the fried chips and place them on absorbent towels to drain. While the chips will stay crisp for an hour or so they should be served as soon as possible.

Makes 48 chips.

SALSAS

Tex-Mex salsas, like so much else in the cuisine, are often less complex than many of those found in Mexico's interior. Often they are made from canned tomatoes, especially the restaurant versions. Although some are quite good, they usually lack the fresh taste of those made from scratch. There are, however, a few that have the best of both worlds: simplicity and freshness.

Following are recipes for a favorite tomato salsa, one made with *tomatillos,* another that is a very good version of restaurant-style salsas, and the ever-popular chile relish, *pico de gallo.*

ROASTED SALSA

During its early years, Tex-Mex cooking was quite similar to that of Mexico's interior, which meant that many of the salsas were made with roasted tomatoes. However, both home cooks and restaurateurs soon learned that less expensive versions could be made with canned tomatoes, and so for many years Tex-Mex restaurants relied on salsas made with them.

Then a San Antonio restaurant called La Fogata (which means The Campfire) opened in what had once been a gas station. It soon became wildly popular serving dishes from Mexico's interior, many of them with roots in the northern states. Their "broiled" salsa was such a hit that it spread throughout the area and is now available in grocery stores. Other Tex-Mex restaurants also began serving it.

This is my favorite salsa, and is certainly one of the easiest to prepare. It is made by broiling tomatoes and *serrano* chiles—you can substitute jalapeños, but I prefer *serranos* for their slightly lemony flavor—until the skins are blackened, then blending them to a puree and straining out the seeds and skins.

In Mexico, cooks often pan broil the tomatoes and chiles on an ungreased griddle, grill or skillet over medium heat. One reason for this is that many Mexicans still do not have ovens with broilers. You can certainly cook them this way, but it requires continually turning the tomatoes and chiles so they will be evenly blackened. I find it much easier to simply place them under a broiler as close as possible to the heat source. For a delightfully smoky flavor you can also broil the tomatoes and chiles over mesquite coals.

The ingredients can be rubbed through an ordinary strainer, but a food mill is a terrific tool and much easier to use.

Hint: You may also place the tomatoes and chiles in the broiler without preheating it, but you will need to add about 5 minutes to the cooking time.

Roasted Salsa

> 4 medium tomatoes
> 2 medium *serrano* or jalapeño chiles
> 1 teaspoon salt, or to taste
> Preheat your oven's broiler.

Place the tomatoes and chiles on a skillet or baking sheet that will withstand high oven heat. Place it under the broiler as close as possible to the heat source and broil until the ingredients are blackened, which will take about 15 minutes.

Place the broiled ingredients in a blender, add the salt, and puree. Push the pureed salsa through a strainer with the back of a spoon or use the fine blade of a food mill.

Serves 4.

SALSA DE TOMATILLOS

(Tomatillo Salsa)

A few restaurants offer more than one salsa with the complimentary chips, and some pair additional salsas with specific menu items. Most often the second salsa will be one made from tomatillos, which are not green tomatoes but the product of an entirely different plant, and from which most Tex-Mex green-chile enchilada sauces are also made.

To save time and money, restaurants often use the same recipe for both their *tomatillo* salsa and their green enchilada sauce, which means that both are cooked. However, a far fresher-tasting version of the salsa is made by simply blending the raw *tomatillos* with the other ingredients.

This salsa, adapted from one presented by Ricardo Muñoz in *Verde en la cocina mexicana,* is extremely easy to prepare, but you must take care to add just the right amount of salt and not over-blend.

Salsa de Tomatillo

3/4 pound fresh *tomatillos,* dry outer husks removed, cut into
    quarters
2 medium-sized *serrano* chiles, stems and seeds removed,
    finely chopped
3 tablespoons chopped white onion
1/2 teaspoon minced garlic
3 tablespoons chopped cilantro
1 heaping teaspoon salt

Place all ingredients in a blender and blend just until the sauce is thick and chunky, but not pureed, about 20 to 25 seconds.

Serves 4.

TEX-MEX RESTAURANT SALSA

Any book on Tex-Mex cooking should have a version of the salsas found in most of the genre's restaurants. The following is a good one.

Tex-Mex Restaurant Salsa

3 large or 4 small jalapeño chiles
2/3 cup water
1 teaspoon white vinegar
Heaping 1/2 teaspoon salt, or to taste
1/4 cup coarsely chopped white onion
1 15-1/2 ounce can whole tomatoes, juice discarded
2 tablespoons chopped cilantro

Cover the jalapeños with water in a small saucepan. Simmer until the chiles are very tender, about 20 minutes. Discard the water and allow the chiles to cool.

When the jalapeños are cool enough to handle, cut off the stem end and, if you wish, remove some or all of the veins and seeds. Removing the veins makes the sauce milder. Removing the seeds does not affect the heat, but does eliminate their unpleasant texture and slightly bitter flavor.

Place the chiles in a blender, add the water, vinegar and salt and blend until pureed. Add the onion, tomatoes and cilantro, and pulse just until the tomatoes are coarsely chopped and combined with the other ingredients.

Serves 4.

PICO DE GALLO
(Chile Relish)

Pico de gallo, which means "rooster's beak," is technically more a relish than a salsa, but is extremely popular in Tex-Mex cooking, especially as a garnish for fajita and other *tacos al carbón*. It is quite easy to prepare, being simply a combination of chopped fresh green chiles (usually *serranos* but sometimes jalapeños), tomato, onion and cilantro, often with a dash of lime juice and salt.

Pico de Gallo

    2 large, ripe tomatoes, cut into 1/4 inch pieces
    3 to 4 *serrano* chiles, very finely chopped
    1/4 cup finely chopped white onion
    1 green onion, finely chopped
    1/4 cup loosely packed, chopped cilantro
    1/4 teaspoon salt (optional)
    1 tablespoon lime juice (optional)

Toss all items together in a small bowl, and serve.

Serves 4.

GUACAMOLE

Somebody once asked, "Why bother with a recipe for guacamole? It's nothing but mashed avocado."

It is true that in Mexico one often finds simple guacamole, just pure avocado mashed with no more than a dash of salt, if that. Indeed, a perfectly ripened avocado can be a work of art by itself. The only thing I can think to compare with its buttery texture and rich, sun-grown flavor is recently pressed, extra-virgin olive oil.

The answer to the question is that as good as a fresh avocado can be unadorned, that is not the only way to make guacamole. It is also not necessarily the best way, particularly if one has avocados that are far from their natural home and have been picked before developing their full flavor.

Tex-Mex restaurants often add other ingredients to their guacamole, not just to create a more interesting flavor combination but also to act as fillers to reduce their food costs. Some also have their wait-staff prepare the guacamole at the table, turning the procedure into an entertaining show.

Probably the most common addition to the avocado is lime juice. It provides a little burst of citrus and helps to retard the avocado's natural deterioration. A variation is to use some of the vinegar from a can of pickled jalapeños. There is no question that a little lime juice or vinegar can certainly help, but many cooks tend to overdo it, as do producers of packaged guacamole who use it to mask their product's less than perfect flavor.

The next most popular additions are salt, followed by minced onion. It is noteworthy that Mexican cooks, including most Tex-Mex cooks, use white onions instead of the sweeter, more watery, yellow onions.

For the best result you should rinse the chopped onion with a little ice water to remove the slightly sulfurous flavor. A little minced *serrano* chile, which has a natural lemony flavor, or jalapeño (fresh or pickled) adds a delightful hint of heat. Cilantro and finely diced tomato round out the additions, and add a nice flavor and texture.

Another way to upgrade your guacamole is to top it with a sprinkling of *cotija, enchilado* or *añejo* cheese. These dry, parmesan-like Mexican cheeses are now available in many parts of the United States. A decent substitute, if used in moderation, is an Italian Romano cheese, which is more salty and stronger in taste than the Mexican cheeses.

Be careful not to over-puree your guacamole. The best way to prevent this is to mash the avocado by hand in a *molcajete* or in a bowl with a fork.

The above provides an idea of just how simple *and* complicated this concoction can be. What I hope you will do is combine some of these ideas with your own to create a personal favorite!

Tex-Mex Guacamole

2 large or 3 to 4 small avocados, peeled and seeded
1/2 teaspoon salt
1/2 tablespoon juice from a can or jar of pickled jalapeño
    chiles
1/2 tablespoon lime juice
1 green onion, minced
2 tablespoons minced white onion
1 tablespoon minced, seeded *serrano* peppers
1/2 cup finely chopped tomato
2 tablespoons minced cilantro

Mash the avocado, then stir in the remaining ingredients.

Serves 4.

NACHOS

I don't know who made the first nacho, but melting some cheese and chile on a tortilla chip is too obvious to believe that the eureka moment was limited to only one cook.

For years nachos were pretty much the same everywhere: thin slices of mild cheddar cheese were placed on tortilla chips topped with slices of pickled jalapeño, and then heated until the cheese melted. From there this simple, delicious appetizer went both up and down the culinary scale. Down in the form of ballpark nachos, a plate of tortilla chips covered in hot, plastic-looking Velveeta, topped with a handful of chopped, pickled jalapeños. At the other end of the scale cooks have added nearly everything to the standard formulation from guacamole to shrimp to something as patently silly as caviar. However, Tex-Mex cooks have created some combinations that enhance the original, and can turn nachos from a taste tempting *botana* into a light meal.

The following is a recipe that will delight, but it is only one of many possibilities. As usual, feel free to unleash your own creativity. Please note that large amounts of nachos can be heated under an oven broiler, and smaller amounts in a microwave. Also, the amount of cheese specified is a bit more than is necessary for home-made tortilla chips, but about right for some of the larger, packaged varieties.

Special Tex-Mex Nachos

24 tortilla chips
1/2 pound grated mild cheddar cheese
1/2 pound grated provolone cheese
1-1/4 cups *picadillo* (see recipe index)
1/3 cup of your favorite salsa
24 1/2-inch pieces of pickled jalapeño
3/4 cup guacamole
24 whole cilantro leaves

Place the chips on a large baking sheet or microwave-safe platter. Mix together the cheddar and provolone and top each one of the chips with some of the mixture. Mix the salsa with the *picadillo* and spoon some of it over the cheese on each chip. If you have any cheese left over, sprinkle it over the *picadillo*, then top each chip with a piece of pickled jalapeño.

Place the nachos either under the broiler or in a microwave. Heat them just until the cheese has melted, no longer or the chips can scorch and the cheese turn gummy. This can take less than a minute, so be careful.

Remove the nachos from the heat source and top each chip with a teaspoon or so of the guacamole. Garnish each with a cilantro leaf and serve.

Makes 24 nachos.

CHILE CON QUESO

Chile con queso means chile with cheese. It is a favorite Tex-Mex appetizer that can be served with tortilla chips or spooned onto and wrapped with flour tortillas. It can also be used as a topping for vegetables, such as potatoes, squash or spinach. In Mexico it is usually made by sautéing chopped onion and poblano chiles, adding and bringing to a boil milk or evaporated milk, then adding pieces of Chihuahua or asadero cheese. These cheeses melt slowly to the consistency of mozzarella, and the dish is usually eaten with tortillas. Sometimes a little chorizo is added with the onions and chiles.

In Tex-Mex cooking, mild cheddar cheese is more common than white cheeses, and the chile of choice is the jalapeño. Unfortunately, some restaurants lower their food cost and preparation time by simply adding some chiles to a cheddar cheese soup concentrate that has been thinned with a little milk or water, or by adding some chiles to melted Velveeta cheese.

The following recipe combines aspects of both the Mexican and Tex-Mex styles, plus a little tequila for added flavor. After all, the Swiss use wines in their fondues, which are quite similar!

The base is made with whole milk and evaporated milk for added richness, and, although fresh chiles will work, canned, pickled jalapeños are used for their extra flavor. The recipe then calls for several different kinds of cheese, which is where you can exercise your own creativity by either changing the proportions or using other cheeses if you wish. Spanish Manchego or Swiss cheeses, although not authentic, are good substitutions.

To keep it warm, Chile con queso can be served in specialized fondue servers or small chafing dishes, or a bowl of it can be placed on electrically-heated serving platters or even on an electric skillet. The key is to keep the heat low enough so the dish does not separate, but hot enough to prevent it from solidifying.

Chile con queso

1 tablespoon plus 1 teaspoon butter
1/2 cup minced white onion
2 pickled jalapeño chiles, stemmed, seeded and minced
    (about 2 1/2 tablespoons)
1/8 teaspoon dried oregano
1/8 teaspoon dried thyme
1/8 teaspoon dried marjoram
2 tablespoons silver tequila
1/3 cup whole milk
1/3 cup evaporated milk
3/4 cup grated mild cheddar cheese
1/2 cup grated provolone cheese
1/2 cup grated Monterey Jack cheese
1/4 cup grated Muenster cheese.

Melt the butter in a saucepan over medium heat, add the onions and chiles and cook until the onions just begin to soften. Add the oregano, thyme, marjoram and tequila and cook an additional minute or two. (If the tequila catches fire, simply shake the pan until the flame goes out.)

Add both milks, turn the heat to high and bring to a rolling boil. Immediately remove the saucepan from the heat, add the cheeses and stir until they are melted; this is necessary as melting the cheese over heat may cause it to separate, making the dish grainy. Serve immediately with tortilla chips or flour tortillas.

Serves 4 as an appetizer.

RICE and BEANS
(Arroz y Frijoles)

Almost all combination plates include a serving of Mexican-style rice and beans—usually, but not always, refried beans—so information about those items and recipes for them are next.

ARROZ MEXICANA
(Mexican Rice)

Arroz mexicana is the pilaf style, tomato-infused rice that accompanies nearly every Tex-Mex meal. It is almost always good, but when properly prepared it is a glorious affair, resembling a minimalist paella.

In the interior of Mexico one sees white rice almost as often as *arroz mexicana* and finds other rices flavored with various herbs and vegetables, as well. However, in Tex-Mex cooking, especially in restaurants, arroz mexicana pretty well sums up the choices. That's all right, because with this style of food it is invariably the perfect accompaniment. The problem is that, in many restaurants, the rice is treated as an afterthought. That is sad because, as noted above, while it may be good, with a little extra time and effort it can be outstanding.

What makes *arroz mexicana* a pilaf-style rice is that the rice is cooked in a little oil before the liquid is added. Following that, the rice is cooked first in some pureed tomato, onion and garlic, then in broth or water. In the process, additional flavors are infused into the rice, making the dish special.

Whether you use water or broth the rice will be very good, but when prepared with a good, home-made chicken broth it is superb. I have tried many different types of rice with this recipe and found that Thai *jasmin* rice produces the best flavor, although Indian *basmati* provides a firmer texture.

Arroz Mexicana

3/4 cup canned, crushed tomatoes
1 large clove garlic, chopped
1/4 cup chopped white onion
2 1/3 cups chicken broth or water
2 cloves garlic, chopped
1 teaspoon salt
1/4 cup olive oil
1 1/2 cups long grain white rice, preferably *jasmin*
1 medium carrot, peeled and shredded
1 cup sliced white onion
1 cup sliced *poblano* chile, or substitute green bell pepper

Blend the crushed tomatoes, 1 clove garlic and onion to a smooth puree and reserve. Blend the broth or water with the 2 cloves garlic and salt for 2 minutes, then reserve.

Heat a 3-quart pot over medium heat and add the 1/4 cup olive oil. When it is hot, stir in the rice, and continue cooking and stirring until it begins to turn golden, reducing the heat as necessary to keep it from burning.

Turn the heat to just over medium, add the reserved tomato puree and cook until most of the liquid has evaporated. You will need to stir it almost constantly until the grains of rice are fairly dry and separate easily, at which time it will be ready for the next step. Turn the heat to high, add the reserved broth mixture, then stir in the carrot, onion and chile or bell pepper. Bring to a boil, stir briefly, cover the pan, turn the heat to very low and cook the rice for 15 minutes.

Remove the rice from the heat and allow it to steam, covered, for 10 minutes. Remove the cover and stir the rice with a fork to separate the grains, then replace the cover and steam for an additional 5 to 10 minutes.

Serves 6 to 8.

FRIJOLES DE OLLA
(Beans from the Pot)

While Tex-Mex cooking usually relies on only one style of rice, it uses nearly every type of bean dish commonly found in Mexico. In different regions in Mexico these dishes are made with different kinds of beans, including black beans, Peruvian beans and bayo beans, but Tex-Mex cooking depends almost exclusively on the pinto bean—which, not surprisingly, is the most popular one in northern Mexico. The recipes begin with *frijoles de olla,* which is the basis for all the other dishes.

Many cooks simply simmer the beans until done, particularly if they will be used as the basis for one of the other, more highly seasoned dishes. But, like so many other items, bean dishes can be improved by adding flavor at each step.

One of the flavors that goes best with pinto beans is pork, usually in the form of lard, bacon or *chorizo.* For this particular dish I suggest a couple slices of bacon, sautéed with a little onion; they will add a great deal to the recipe and to any that follow. Another flavor that works well is garlic.

Rather than adding garlic to the cooking beans, I prefer to add it with the cooking water. To do this, in a blender add 3 to 4 cloves of garlic to about 3/4 cup water and blend until totally pureed. Then fill the blender with additional water and re-blend. (It is easier to puree the garlic in a small amount of water).

One thing that speeds up the cooking process is to cook the beans in just enough water to cover them by an inch or so, then add in small amounts of additional hot liquid as needed, as opposed to using a large quantity of water at the beginning. If the beans are cooked at a very low simmer their skins will tend to remain attached and they will generally remain more intact. Cooking them vigorously causes the skins to come off, which creates a thicker sauce.

The former is a more sophisticated outcome, and the latter more rustic. Although both styles are common in Tex-Mex cooking, I prefer the rustic method, but you should try it both ways and suit yourself. Always add the salt at the end, when the beans are tender.

A word of caution: Soak the beans for a minute or two during the cleaning process in order to remove all dirt, and dissolve any bits of mud. Yes, you can find it in even the cleanest-looking package!

Frijoles de Olla

1 pound pinto beans, well-cleaned, briefly soaked, and picked
over
4 cloves garlic, peeled and coarsely chopped
1/2 tablespoon olive oil
2 slices bacon, finely chopped
1/2 cup finely chopped white onion
1/2 teaspoon oregano
1/4 teaspoon powdered cumin
1 teaspoon salt, or to taste

Clean the beans thoroughly and set them aside. Blend the garlic with about 3/4 cup water until completely pureed, 1 to 2 minutes. Add enough water to total 4 cups, blend again and reserve. Heat a large pot over medium heat, add the oil and bacon, and cook until the bacon is just cooked through and beginning to render its fat.

Add the onion and continue cooking until it is soft but not browned. Add the beans and the 4 cups garlic-infused water from the blender. Bring to a simmer, add the oregano and cumin and cook, partially covered, for about 10 minutes. Continue cooking, adding water as necessary until the beans are tender and just barely covered with liquid.

The exact cooking time and amount of liquid depend on your altitude, how dry the beans were and to what extent the pot is covered, but usually the process takes 1 hour 20 to 30 minutes and a total of 8 to 9 cups of liquid. Add the salt just before the beans are done.

Serves 6-8.

FRIJOLES BORRACHOS
(Drunken Beans)

As in other cuisines, the word "drunken" in a Mexican recipe's name signifies that it contains alcohol in one form or another. In central and southern Mexico, *frijoles borrachos* is often made with pulque, a mild beer-like liquor made from the same basic plant as tequila and mescal, but in northern Mexico and in Tex-Mex cooking beer is the usual choice. Fortunately you do not have to be of legal age to enjoy this dish, because the vast majority of the alcohol evaporates during the cooking process. These beans are traditionally served at cookouts with meats cooked *al carbón* (char-broiled).

Frijoles Borrachos

To make *frijoles borrachos* use the recipe for *frijoles de olla.* Start the beans, as usual, with 4 cups of garlic-infused water, then add 2 12-ounce bottles (3 cups) beer (instead of water), then add more water as necessary. It's that simple!
Serves 6 to 8.

FRIJOLES RANCHEROS or FRIJOLES a la CHARRA

(Ranch or Horsewoman-style Beans)

These two recipes are virtually the same, and are made by adding a sauce of tomato, onion and chiles to either *frijoles de olla* or *frijoles borrachos* just before they are done. For this dish I suggest adding some *chorizo*. Yes, another pork fat on top of the bacon, but one that produces a great deal of flavor. I also suggest using crushed tomatoes, as they make an assertive complement to the strong flavor of the beans and *chorizo*.

Frijoles Rancheros or Frijoles a la Charra

1 recipe *frijoles de olla* or *frijoles borrachos*
1 tablespoon olive oil
1/3 cup crumbled Mexican *chorizo*
3 *serrano* or jalapeño chiles, stemmed, seeded and finely
    chopped
1 cup chopped white onions
3/4 cup canned crushed tomatoes
1/2 cup loosely packed, chopped cilantro
1 teaspoon salt, or to taste

Heat the cooked beans to just below a simmer. Place a skillet over medium heat, add the oil, then add the chorizo and cook, stirring constantly, until it begins to brown.

Add the chiles and onions and continue cooking until the onions are soft but not browned. Add the crushed tomatoes and continue cooking until the mixture begins to thicken, then add the cilantro and cook another minute.

Add the sauce to the beans, bring them to a low simmer, add the salt, and continue cooking them for another 5 minutes.

Serves 6 to 8.

FRIJOLES REFRITOS
(Refried Beans)

You can make decent refried beans using olive or another vegetable oil, but only pork fat, in one form another, usually lard, will produce great refried beans. Many Tex-Mex cooks use bacon fat or fry the beans with some chorizo. I suggest you use either homemade lard (see index) or bacon fat mixed with some olive oil.

In terms of other seasonings, if you are making your refried beans from the *frijoles de olla* in this book they will have plenty of flavor, although I like to add a little more powdered cumin. You can also make refried beans from either canned pinto beans or by heating a can of refried beans—as do many Tex-Mex cooks at home—but they will not be nearly as good.

I heartily recommend serving refried beans with a sprinkling of *cotija* or *añejo* cheese on top. The two go together like popcorn and butter.

In most cases, Tex-Mex dishes can be prepared without the need to use specific Mexican cheeses, but in this case there is no substitute for the mild Mexican cheese that somewhat resembles Parmesan in texture (although some cooks do use grated mild cheddar cheese). Fortunately it is widely available in well-stocked super markets and Hispanic specialty stores.

Hint: The following recipe calls for pureeing the cooked beans in a food processor before frying them. If you wish to do it the old fashioned way, simply add the whole beans to the pan with some broth, then mash them with a potato masher.

Frijoles Refritos

2 1/2 cups *frijoles de olla* strained, and their broth reserved
2 1/2 tablespoons lard or a combination of bacon fat and olive oil

24

Heaping 1/4 teaspoon powdered cumin
1/2 cup grated *cotija* or *añejo* cheese (optional)

If you are using the food processor method, place the beans in the bowl with the steel blade. Turn on the machine and slowly add just enough of the bean's cooking liquid to allow a medium puree, one that still has a few lumps in it. If you do not have enough cooking liquid, use water.

Heat a skillet over medium to medium-high heat and add the lard. When the lard has melted, add the pureed beans (or whole beans and about 1/2 cup of their liquid, if you choose this method) and the cumin, and cook, stirring constantly (or mashing the beans with a potato masher) until they are heated through and no longer runny. Be careful, though, as they can quickly overcook, which will make them dry and grainy. If that begins to happen just add a little more bean liquid or water.

Serve the beans and top each portion with about 2 tablespoons of the cheese, if you wish.

Serves 4.

WRAPS, FILLINGS AND ANTOJITOS

In Mexico, *antojitos* is the word used to describe typical light meals and snacks, such as enchiladas, tacos and tamales. In English the word translates appropriately to "little whims." One good way of explaining *antojitos* is to say that they consist of a wrap, a filling and a sauce and/or garnish. To illustrate, a taco uses a corn or flour tortilla as a wrap to enclose a filling, usually one made of ground or shredded meat. The filling, enclosed in its wrap, is then garnished with one or more ingredients such as salsa, lettuce, tomato, cheese or guacamole.

One of the secrets of Mexican cooking is that many of the wraps, fillings and garnishes for *antojitos* are interchangeable. For example, the same filling may be used for tacos, enchiladas, and *flautas* and they are all wrapped with tortillas. The result is that by preparing just a few fillings, sauces and garnishes, and combining them with tortillas in various shapes and textures, restaurants or home cooks can present nearly an entire menu from a relatively few basic items. Therefore we begin this section with recipes for the most important wraps, fillings, sauces (as opposed to salsas) and garnishes, then proceed to the *antojitos*, themselves for these are the most important components of the Tex-Mex combination plate.

WRAPS: TORTILLAS

Tortillas serve as the staff of life in Mexico, the way most *norte americanos* think of bread. They come in two basic types, depending on their main ingredient: corn and flour.

In central and southern Mexico the corn tortillas developed by the earliest inhabitants are king of the hill. These "little corn cakes," so described by John

Steinbeck on an early trip to Baja California, are also popular in northern Mexico and in Tex-Mex cooking, where they are essential for making enchiladas, crispy tacos, nachos, *flautas, tostadas* and, of course, the ever-popular tortilla chips.

However, when Spaniards arrived in Mexico they brought wheat seed with them, intending to produce their staple, bread. But in the heat and humidity of southern Mexico the crop fared poorly, and the Spaniards quickly adopted the Indians' delicious corn tortillas as their own.

When Spanish settlers reached northern Mexico they discovered that wheat thrived in the region's dry air and cold winters. But so accustomed had they become to tortillas that instead of using wheat flour to make bread, they fashioned it into a new type of tortilla. It soon became apparent that *tortillas de harina*—flour tortillas—had several advantages over those made of corn. Flour tortillas were easier to prepare, could be made much larger and did not spoil nearly as quickly. So they were an ideal wrap for the dried beef that cowboys on the vast northern ranchos carried to sustain themselves during the work day. The result is that in northern Mexico corn tortillas share top billing with tortillas made of wheat flour, and that is where Tex-Mex originates.

CORN TORTILLAS

There is a significant difference between the corn tortillas found in Mexico and those in the United States. Those from Mexico's interior are moist with a soft spongy texture and perfumed with the essence of fresh corn. They are sold in small tortilla factories located in nearly every neighborhood and within many supermarkets. Because they begin to spoil within hours after being prepared, corn tortillas are made and bought fresh each day.

While there are a fair number of such tortilla factories in South Texas cities, they are far from city-wide. Outside the Southwest, tortilla factories, although increasing in number, can still be few and far between. Even in places like San Antonio most families purchase their tortillas at supermarkets, where most of them come from huge, often distant factories. To keep them fresh and from sticking together, these commercial tortillas may contain preservatives and are made with less water, making them much dryer than most of those found in Mexico's interior.

Besides being dryer—sometimes to the point of resembling cardboard— they are also thinner than most of those in Mexico. While being dryer and thin- ner often makes our tortillas unsuitable to be used as a substitute for bread, as they are in Mexico, they are not all bad, as we shall see.

The dough for corn tortillas is still made by cooking dried corn kernels in an alkaline solution derived from lime, ashes or seashells. The process makes it possible to remove the tough skins before grinding them into a smooth masa or dough the Aztecs called *nixtamal.*

It is historically important—not to mention amazing—that, in addition to allowing the skins to be removed and a smooth dough to be made, the process- ing by which corn is turned into nixtamal also provides the key to unlocking corn's nutrition by allowing the body to absorb critical nutrients. Not realizing this, when the first European explorers discovered corn and sent it around the world they neglected to include this process. Thus, people from Africa to the American South attempting to subsist on corn became ill and sometimes died from a disease called pellagra. It was not until late in the twentieth century that scientists fully understood the genius of the early Indians, and were able to solve the mystery. What is astounding is that this life-enabling chemical process called nixtamalization was discovered thousands of years ago by Mexico's earli- est inhabitants, and has only recently been fully understood.

Originally this *masa* was then patted by hand into thin circles and cooked on clay *comales* (griddles). In modern tortilla factories the dough is pressed out by machine onto a conveyer belt passing over gas flames that bake the tortillas.

In many cases *nixtamal* is dried and ground into a flour, to which water is added to form the dough. This may make the manufacturing process more hygienic but it produces tortillas not quite as rich in natural corn flavor, and with a texture that is less elastic. These corn flours are available in most U.S. supermarkets under the names MaSeca and Masa Harina.

Not surprisingly, most Tex-Mex recipes are designed to be made with the dryer, thinner supermarket corn tortillas found in this country. When fried they produce a lighter, crisper result than the more moist, interior variety. For that reason and because making good corn tortillas is a bit of a chore, I suggest you purchase them whenever possible. As more and more immigrants from Mexico settle outside the southwest, more and more supermarkets in other parts of the country are stocking this staple.

Corn Tortillas

If decent corn tortillas are simply not available you can make them with either MaSeca or Masa Harina. Simply follow the directions on the package to make the dough and allow it to re-hydrate for about half an hour. Separate the dough into 6 pieces for each 1 cup of corn flour you use to make it, and roll each piece into a smooth ball.

To form the dough, place a ball of it between small sheets of wax paper and flatten it in a tortilla press. Remove the top piece of wax paper and place the uncooked tortilla, exposed dough-side, down on the palm of one hand. Peel off the remaining piece of wax paper and, with a sweeping motion, slide the dough onto an ungreased skillet or griddle preheated over medium heat. An even easier method is to press the balls of dough in an electric tortilla or flatbread maker. These devices both form and cook the dough. Turn the tortillas over once or twice until cooked through.

FLOUR TORTILLAS

Flour tortillas are very popular in the United States, especially in the Southwest where they are widely available in supermarkets. No doubt much of this popularity derives from the fact that our border with Mexico touches the northern states where flour tortillas were invented, and from whence a large percentage of Mexican immigrants come to this country. Flour tortillas are also popular because really good home-style corn tortillas are difficult to find in the United States, and top quality flour tortillas are relatively easy to make.

All flour tortillas are similar in ingredients but not in size. They vary from about 4 inches to about 18 inches in diameter, and in thickness from paper-thin to over 1/8 inch thick. Generally, the largest, thinnest tortillas are found in the Mexican state of Sonora, where burritos are thought to have been invented. This style is also popular in Baja California and in Arizona, California and New Mexico. The exception is Tex-Mex cooking where thick, puffy flour tortillas are used in place of bread and to wrap fajitas and other fillings.

The most common size, and the one most used in South Texas, is what I call the all-purpose flour tortilla. It has a diameter of about 6 to 7 inches and is about 1/8 inch thick.

Ingredients and techniques:

Flour tortillas are made with wheat flour, a fat, salt and water. Some cooks also add a little baking powder.

Flour:

In Mexico most of the flour is fairly soft, which means it is lower in protein and gluten—the elements that give bread its elastic quality—than bread flour but higher than cake flour. Our all-purpose flours are a good substitute and are excellent for flour tortillas. Some commercial bakeries in the United States use a harder, bread-type flour with more protein and gluten, and the result is tortillas with a texture so rubbery that they turn taking a bite into a tug of war.

The fat:

Lard is the traditional fat used to make flour tortillas and is still my favorite, although those made in Sonora with rendered beef fat have a very special flavor as well. If you do not wish to use supermarket lard, simply make your own using the following recipe.

Many cooks use shortening in their tortillas. However, I find that such tortillas have no real flavor, and there is the disadvantage that the shortening is hydrogenated. As mentioned earlier, some cooks in Sonora use rendered beef fat, which can be made the same way as lard. Although few Tex-Mex cooks use it, I find that a neutral oil, such as canola oil, makes a good alternative to lard.

Regarding the amount of fat, the rule of thumb is around 1 1/2 tablespoons per cup of flour, although commercial producers often use much less. In fact, reasonably good flour tortillas can be successfully made with as little as 1/2 tablespoon fat per cup of flour. Remember that tortillas made with more fat will have more flavor but will become stiff and hard when refrigerated.

Lard:

These days it is common for people to recoil in horror like a vampire confronted by a cross at the very mention of the word "lard," but lard is an essential ingredient for both flour tortillas and tamales. It is important to remember that good quality lard actually has less saturated fat than butter. Many nutrition experts maintain that hydrogenated fats such as those found in margarine and shortening are more dangerous to health than the saturated fats found in butter and lard.

But good quality lard does not include the products found in most supermarkets. That lard is usually hydrogenated and otherwise preserved to the point that, like shortening, it does not require refrigeration. Is there not some small voice that whispers to you that something is wrong with an animal fat product that does not need refrigeration?

If you do not have access to good lard you can make your own. It will be pure, tasty, home-made lard and will require refrigeration. A quick and easy way to produce small quantities, but one that requires caution because of the extreme heat and steam involved, is as follows: place 1/3 cup diced pork fat in a 2-cup Pyrex measuring cup, cover it with good quality plastic wrap and microwave it on high, a minute at a time, until most of the fat is melted and any bits of meat just begin to brown. It usually takes a total of 2 to 3 minutes. Allow the fat to cool slightly, and strain the liquid into a sterile jar. Repeat the process until you have as much lard as you wish.

The only downside to this approach is that it makes relatively small quantities and you must take great care to avoid touching the glass container and the steam that is released when the plastic wrap is removed. I always use gloves made for handling hot objects and kitchen tongs to remove the plastic wrap.

For large quantities I suggest you use the method advocated by Diana Kennedy. Place 1 pound pork fat, cut into very small pieces, in an oven-proof skillet or baking dish, more or less in one layer, and place it in an oven preheated to 325 degrees. Cook until the fat begins to render and pour it through a strainer into a large jar or other suitable container. Continue cooking and pouring off the melted lard until the fat begins to brown. Allow the strained lard to cool, then refrigerate.

Baking powder:

Many cooks add a little baking powder to their flour tortilla dough. After much trial and error I have concluded that its use is largely unnecessary for thin tortillas, but does have some effect on the thick, pillow-like Tex-Mex variety, making them slightly more puffy and lighter.

Making the dough:

When making the dough, solid fat, whether lard or butter or a combination, can be added in a warm but still solid state. I find it much easier to melt the fat with the water, allow it to cool slightly, then add the two ingredients together in a stream. Using the hot liquid also seems to make the tortillas softer. The result is a uniform dispersal of the fat and a very pliable dough.

The dough can be mixed by hand or made in a food processor fitted with the steel blade by pouring the liquid and melted fat slowly into the dry ingredients, after turning on the machine, until a ball of dough just begins to form. Do not over-process.

Shaping the dough:

Flour tortillas can be made with the standard, large rolling pins, but a better choice is a smaller, solid wooden one. In Mexico and Texas special pins are sold just for flour tortillas. A 1 1/4-inch-diameter wooden dowel cut to 14 inches in length works well as a substitute.

Before forming the tortillas, divide the dough into balls and allow them to rest for about 10 minutes. This will permit the gluten to relax and will make the tortillas much easier to form.

To form the tortillas, roll the dough balls, turning them clockwise or counter clockwise a little as you do so and turning them over onto the other side after about every third roll.

Low-fat alternative:

For those interested in making decent flour tortillas with a minimum of fat, prepare the basic recipe that follows with 1 tablespoon of canola oil. Mix the oil with very warm tap water before adding it to the flour. The result is a very soft tortilla with a nice, light texture and low fat content.

Basic Flour Tortilla Recipe

The following recipe is meant to serve as a standard, from which readers are encouraged to experiment based on their own taste and dietary requirements, particularly in terms of the type and amount of fat.

2 cups all-purpose flour
1/2 teaspoon salt
Heaping 1/4 teaspoon baking powder
3 tablespoons good-quality lard or other fat (see above)
2/3 cup water

Mix the flour, salt and baking powder either in a bowl or in a food processor fitted with the steel blade. Heat the water and lard or other fat over low heat, or in a microwave at high heat until the lard has just melted. Gradually stir the liquid into the flour and form into a dough by hand, or pour into the processor with the motor running.

The result should be a dough that is neither wet nor dry and crumbly. If it seems too wet, add a little more flour; or if too dry, add a little more water.

Knead the dough briefly, then divide it into 10 pieces. Roll the pieces of dough into little balls between the palms of your hands, then cover them with a slightly damp towel and allow them to rest for at least 10 minutes and up to an hour and a half. This will allow the gluten to relax and make them easier to shape.

Roll the dough into rounds 6 to 7 inches in diameter and about 1/8-inch thick using the technique described above. Meanwhile, heat a large, heavy skillet or griddle over medium heat. Since stove settings vary you will have to experiment to find the best heat for your particular situation.

When the skillet or griddle has preheated, place one of the rolled dough pieces on it. Within about 30 seconds it should start to bubble and some little brown spots begin to form on the bottom. Flip the tortilla over and cook another 30 seconds.

By this time it should start to puff, and the other side will develop light brown spots. Flip the tortilla again, at which time it should immediately begin to puff more, sometimes into a large, nearly round ball. When the tortilla has fully expanded, remove it from the heat and place it in a tortilla warmer or wrap it in a thick towel, where it will deflate.

As you proceed, adjust the heat based on the above description. For example, reduce the heat if after about 30 seconds the bottom of the tortilla is beginning to char, or raise it if nothing much has happened. Repeat the process for the remaining tortillas.

Makes 10 tortillas.

FILLINGS:
GROUND to SHREDDED

Picadillo
(Ground-Beef Filling)

One of the major differences between Tex-Mex cooking and that of
Mexico's interior is that instead of using the shredded-meat fillings
that are so common in Mexico, Tex-Mex cooks more often use
ground meat fillings. In Spanish the word *picadillo* (peek-ah-dee-oh) is used to
describe these fillings. They are usually pretty basic, normally made by frying
ground beef with a little chile powder, garlic, cumin, oregano and salt for a few
minutes.

In Mexico, tacos are usually filled with shredded beef, but when a *picadillo*
is used they are often more elaborate. In addition to chile powder, garlic, cumin,
oregano and salt, cooks will often include aromatics such as cinnamon, cloves
and allspice. They also often add water and simmer the dish until it evaporates.
This is done to make the flavors more subtle, and the meat texture smoother
and more tender. Remember, most ground beef is made from tough cuts such
as the chuck and the round, and even though they are finely ground they can
still be a bit chewy.

Interior Mexican and some Tex-Mex cooks often include finely chopped
potato. The starch helps bind the filling. During the cooking process the bits of
potato melt into the other ingredients, adding an even smoother texture and
additional flavor. While the more elaborate *picadillo*s have found their way into
some Tex-Mex homes, they rarely end up in restaurants as they require more
time and ingredients. "If the market doesn't demand it, why go to the extra
trouble and expense?" is the usual reasoning.

The following recipe is designed to be used to prepare a simple *picadillo* in
about ten minutes, or a much more complex and delicious one in about an
hour and a quarter. I suggest that you try the recipe with all the options, then

modify it to suit your own taste and available time. I think you will agree that the more elaborate version is the best and worth the extra time and effort.

All-Purpose Picadillo

1 tablespoon olive oil
1 pound 85% lean ground beef
2 cloves garlic, peeled and finely chopped
3/4 teaspoon pure *ancho* chile powder
1 teaspoon dried, leaf oregano
1/4 teaspoon ground cumin
3/4 teaspoon salt or to taste
1/4 teaspoon ground cloves (optional)
1/4 teaspoon ground allspice (optional)
 1/4 teaspoon ground cinnamon (optional)
3 cups water (optional)
1 cup russet potato, peeled and cut to 1/4-inch dice (optional)

Heat the oil in a medium saucepan over medium heat. Add the ground beef and fry, stirring constantly until it is cooked through. Add the garlic, chile powder, oregano, cumin and salt. At this point you have a very simple *picadillo* that only needs a few more minutes of cooking to be completed.

If desired, add the optional cloves, allspice and cinnamon and continue cooking, stirring constantly, for about two minutes. You now have a very simple version of a more complex filling.

For the ultimate version, add the water and stir in the potatoes. Bring to a bare simmer and cook, adjusting the heat as necessary, until the liquid has evaporated and the filling is thick, tender and smooth, about 1 hour and 15 minutes. You can also add less water and cook for a shorter period of time if you wish. In this regard it is worthwhile to note the changes in the filling as it cooks and to determine the time you think is optimal.

Chorizo and Potato Filling

With only two ingredients and a very simple cooking process, this is one of the easiest Tex-Mex fillings to make, and is delicious in tacos, *flautas* and *tostadas*

1/3 cup peeled potato, cut into 1/4 inch dice
Cooking oil
3/4 pound *chorizo*

Place the cut-up potato in a small saucepan, cover with 2 inches with water, bring to a boil and simmer until the potatoes are just cooked through. Pour the potatoes into a strainer, discarding the cooking water. Then pour cold water over the potatoes until they are cool enough to keep them from continuing to cook.

Heat a skillet over medium heat, add just enough oil to coat the pan, then add the *chorizo*. Continue cooking, breaking the chorizo into small pieces, until it is just cooked through. Add the potatoes and continue cooking until the chorizo is beginning to crisp and the potatoes are beginning to brown.

Shredded-Beef Filling

Ground meat fillings or *picadillos* are the favorite fillings in Tex-Mex cooking because immigrants discovered that hamburger meat was the most economical cut. But in Mexico fillings made from whole pieces of meat that are cooked and shredded are still, by far, most often used. Many Tex-Mex cooks still prefer this type.

Leftover cooked meats of any kind can be shredded and used as a filling, including the recipes for country-style spareribs and *carnitas*, but most often beef is the choice. If you are making a shredded-beef filling from scratch, I suggest you use a well-trimmed beef brisket. Because this cut is so grainy it more easily shreds into long, thin pieces. In fact, in Mexico brisket is often referred to as *carne para deshebrar*, or "meat for shredding." You can also use other cuts such as the rump, but it does not make sense to use more expensive pieces such as sirloin.

While most brisket in Texas consists of the extremely large and fatty market cut used to make barbecued brisket, in other parts of the country a smaller, trimmed portion is most popular. Pick a piece around 2 pounds. The meat can be cut into 1 or 2 inch chunks, which will speed up the cooking process, but I suggest you leave it in one piece. And while most cooks simply place the meat in a pot and simmer it until tender, I prefer to first brown it in cooking oil. The result is much more juicy, and the browned portions add a lot more flavor to whatever you will be using it for.

Hint: You can simmer the meat on top of the stove, but it is much easier to place it in a low oven, which will ensure it will be cooked at the proper temperature as too vigorous a boil will make the meat dry and tough.

Shredded-Beef Filling

1/4 cup cooking oil
About 2 pounds beef brisket, or another cut

Preheat your oven to 300 degrees. Place the oil in a large, oven-usable pot over medium high to high heat. When it just begins to smoke, add the meat, and leave it until it is thoroughly browned, about 1 to 1 1/2 minutes. Turn the meat and brown it on the other side.

Remove the pot from the heat and add enough water to cover

the meat. Replace the pot on the burner and bring the liquid to a simmer over high heat. Skim the surface, cover the pot, and put it into the oven.

After 2 hours, check the meat. If it is very tender, remove it; if not, continue to cook it for another half hour. When the meat is done, remove the pot from the oven, and allow it to cool for about 1 hour, still covered.

When the meat has cooled, shred it, discarding any remaining fat. One simple way to do this is to cut it into two-inch chunks and process in batches in a food processor, using the dough blade.

You may wish to save the broth from the pot. If so, refrigerate it, then remove any congealed fat from the surface.

Makes 4 to 5 cups shredded beef filling.

Shredded-Chicken Filling

How you make this filling will depend on whether you like light or dark meat, and how much time you have. If you prefer light meat use the breast, if you like dark meat use the thighs. If you like both, use a whole chicken.

If you are in a hurry, you can boil boned cuts until they are cooked through, about 10 to 15 minutes, but the result will not be nearly as tender. You will get far better results by simmering pieces complete with the bones and skin for an hour. It will be much more tender, and if you add some onion, garlic and carrots to the pot you will have a very nice broth. In fact, this is how the fresh chicken soup found in the next section is made.

Shredded chicken can be dry, especially if it is made with boneless, skinless breasts. To solve this problem, after the meat has been shredded place it in a bowl and add enough broth to moisten it. As the meat will absorb some of the liquid, keep adding broth until it refuses to absorb more. Leave just a little excess liquid in with the chicken, to ensure that when you use it it will be moist.

The following gives a general guide to how much shredded meat per pound of uncooked chicken you will obtain from various cuts in terms of both weight and volume.

1 pound bone-in breasts yields about 8 ounces of shredded meat, or 1 1/2 cups

1 pound bone-in thighs yields about 8 ounces of shredded meat, or about 1 1/4 cups

1 pound drumsticks yields about 6 ounces of shredded meat, or about 1 1/8 cups

A 2 3/4 pound chicken yields about 12 ounces of shredded white meat, about 2 1/4 cups, and about 12 ounces of shredded dark meat, about 2 cups

Shredded-Chicken Filling

To make the shredded chicken, place whatever amount and type of chicken you choose (see chart, above) in a stockpot, cover it with water by at least 2 inches, add some chunks of onion and carrot and a few cloves of crushed garlic. Bring the liquid to a boil, skim off the scum that rises to the surface, replace some of the water you removed, then simmer it gently for one hour. Allow the chicken to cool for at least 1 hour in the broth.

You can remove the chicken, discard the skin and bones and shred the meat at this time or you can leave it in the pot and refrigerate over night, remove the congealed fat from the broth and shred the meat the next day.

Other Fillings

The recipes for both country-style spareribs and carnitas make terrific fillings. Simply prepare them then either shred or finely chop the meat.

ANTOJITOS:
ENCHILADAS to GORDITAS

Following are recipes for the main event of the Tex-Mex combination plate, the tortilla-wrapped specialties that include enchiladas and tacos and the other treats that have made this cuisine so popular.

ENCHILADAS

The word "enchilada" comes from the Spanish verb *enchilar,* which is translated "to add chile to." A secondary definition is "to annoy," but for our purposes that only applies to greenhorns with tender palates.

The exact place of enchiladas in the Texas food pantheon was probably best described by a salty West Texan who noted, "Tacos is snackin' food and enchiladas is dinner food." What he meant is that while tacos are often eaten casually as a snack or light meal, enchiladas are usually part of more formal dining.

Indeed, enchiladas have become a part of South Texas culture. In addition to being the main attraction of the combination plates in Tex-Mex restaurants, enchiladas are the traditional school lunch on Wednesdays in San Antonio. And to this day enchiladas are the center of a South Texas controversy that can reach epic proportions. The point of contention is whether or not they should be garnished with raw onions.

Whether you decide to have onions or not, as you sit down to a plate of enchiladas it is interesting to reflect on the fact that you are enjoying something that is the culmination of over 2,000 years of culinary experimentation. That they have changed so little over time is a testimonial to the wisdom of whoever dipped the first corn tortilla into chile sauce.

From a culinary standpoint, an enchilada is no more complicated than a corn tortilla bathed in chile sauce, then folded or wrapped with or without a filling. That is probably how the first enchilada was fashioned a thousand or more years before Hernan Cortés conquered Mexico.

Traditionally, enchiladas are classified as red or green, referring to the color of the chiles used to make the sauce. Red chile sauces are made with dried chiles, with the *ancho* chile being the most popular one in Tex-Mex cooking. Red chile sauces (see recipe index) are made by re-hydrating the chiles, blending them with water or broth and spices, including garlic, oregano, cumin and salt, then sometimes cooking them in oil or lard until they thicken.

In Mexico this is usually the end of the process, but on this side of the border, and certainly in Tex-Mex cooking, cooks almost always simmer the sauce, adding additional liquid, usually a mild beef broth, then thickening it with a flour-based roux. More importantly, instead of simply serving the freshly-dipped tortillas wrapped around a filling of meat or cheese as they do in Mexico, Tex-Mex cooks invariably submerge the enchiladas in sauce, add liberal amounts of cheese, then heat the plate to a glorious, bubbling inferno: "Hot plate, *señor!*"

Green chile sauces and the enchiladas made from them are quite similar on both sides of the border. They are made with fresh chiles, usually *serrano*s or *poblano*s, that are usually simmered with tomatillos until soft, then blended with garlic, onion, salt and sometimes cilantro, then cooked in a little oil or lard until thickened. The major difference is that in this country, as with red chile enchiladas, the plate is often given a final blast in the oven. In Tex-Mex cooking, enchiladas are sometimes also served with a *ranchero* sauce, *(see recipe index)* made by simmering jalapeño or *serrano* chiles with tomatoes and onions.

On most combination plates the enchilada lies buried beneath a sea of molten red chile sauce and melted cheese. It is surrounded perhaps by a tamale and taco but certainly by steaming portions of Mexican rice, refried beans and often a garnish of shredded lettuce. But regardless of the number or type of "accessories," it is the enchilada with its earthy, soul-nourishing chile sauce that anchors this deceptively simple, spectacularly popular dish.

43

As we have learned, the Tex-Mex tradition comes from immigrants who came to work on the ranches and later in the cities of South Texas, where they joined the larger community. They found that, unlike in Mexico, virtually every kitchen included an oven. This made it possible to prepare enchiladas in advance, then add the sauce at the last minute before heating and serving.

Tex-Mex enchilada sauces are like no others in that they are made with either beef or beef broth and contain, in comparison to other styles, substantial amounts of cumin. They also often include some tomato in one form or another. As with other *antojitos mexicanos,* enchiladas consist of a wrap (corn tortillas), a filling (in Tex-Mex cooking usually either cheese, *picadillo,* shredded beef, or shredded chicken) and a garnish (one of the Tex-Mex red chile sauces, or green chile sauce or ranchero sauce).

We could have written out enchilada recipes for each of these alternatives, but thought it more efficient to include them in one basic recipe. More important, this approach emphasizes the possible combinations of the three elements involved. We will take a quick look at each before going on to a one-size-fits-all recipe.

The wrap:

Tex-Mex enchiladas are always wrapped with corn tortillas that have been briefly immersed in hot oil to make them both flexible and less likely to absorb their sauce and become mushy.

The traditional way to do this is to heat about half an inch of cooking oil in a small skillet over medium heat. It should be hot enough so that when a tortilla is immersed it immediately begins to cook vigorously.

Using tongs, place a tortilla in the oil and allow it to cook for about 15 to 20 seconds, without allowing it to become crisp. It should be very soft and pliable, so adjust your heat accordingly.

Remove the tortilla from the oil and place it on absorbent towels to drain. Prepare the remaining tortillas in the same fashion.

A much easier and less messy way is to use a microwave, and that method is described in the recipe that follows.

The filling:

The principal fillings for Tex-Mex enchiladas are cheese, *picadillo*, shredded beef and shredded chicken.

Many of the cheeses used for enchiladas in Mexico are now available in this country. However, since Tex-Mex cooking evolved before they found their way to our markets, easily found supermarket cheeses are perfect for all the recipes. In fact, since low price and availability were prime considerations in early Tex-Mex kitchens, most cooks used—and many still use—yellow cheeses, including Velveeta, American or mild cheddar.

I do not recommend the first alternative. No amount of authenticity mitigates the gummy, plastic texture, but a good mild cheddar is perfect, sometimes mixed with a little mozzarella to provide a contrast of color, flavor and texture. Although not used as often, I like to combine a little smoked provolone with one of the others; it adds a touch of its smoky taste to the dish.

Whatever cheese you use, please note that the ones that come already grated in plastic packages never seem to be as good as when you buy the bulk cheese and grate it yourself, easily done with a food processor.

Recipes for *picadillo*, shredded beef and chicken fillings can be found in the recipe index.

Each tortilla should be filled with about 3/4 ounce, about 2 tablespoons of one of these fillings.

The sauce and garnish:

Tex-Mex enchiladas are most often covered with red chile sauce, but green chile sauce and *ranchero* sauce are also popular. Recipes for the red and green chile sauces follow this explanation. (See index for *Ranchero* sauce recipe.)

Regardless of the type of sauce used, Tex-Mex enchiladas are invariably garnished with cheese, usually a yellow cheese, of which a mild cheddar is my favorite. Sometimes a white cheese, such as mozzarella or provolone is used, especially with green chile sauces, and quite often a white and yellow cheese are mixed to provide contrasts of taste, texture and color.

TEX-MEX RED CHILE ENCHILADA SAUCE

To most Texans, Tex-Mex food is an important part of their culture. For more than a few, the passion for it goes beyond a mere treat to something that verges on being—dare we even whisper it—addictive.

More often than not, Texans get their fix at a favorite restaurant. It is usually the house's signature red chile enchilada sauce that gives them their high. This meaty, chile-infused gravy with a bite of cumin, a touch of Mexican oregano and a hint of aromatic garlic is the prime element in Tex-Mex style enchiladas and combination plates. Like lava flowing through a village, it submerges the enchiladas and gently laps around the rice, beans, taco and tamale, or whatever else is included.

It is the enchantingly earthy smell of this sauce, together with that of steaming corn tortillas, that greets customers as they approach the restaurant and keeps them returning, time after time. If you are a regular customer and ask politely, your favorite Tex-Mex restaurateur will usually give you the recipe for just about anything on the menu except the red chile enchilada sauce. While he or she may reluctantly divulge the ingredients (at least some of them), the proportions and process that would actually allow you to make that addictive concoction remain carefully guarded secrets, for these are truly secret sauces whose recipes are closely guarded by generations of family members.

These sauces, in addition to the use of ground rather than shredded meat and yellow instead of white cheese, are what distinguishes the Mexican cooking on this side of the border from that of Mexico's interior. It took me a long time and a lot of trial and error with many wrong turns to get to this, the center of the Tex-Mex universe. It is important for cooks to understand the process so that they can make appropriate modifications and create their own very best version. Although easy to prepare, these sauces are far from simple, with as many subtleties as any sauce in any cuisine.

The following recipe specifies whole *ancho* chiles. If you are determined to use chile powder, substitute 1 tablespoon for each chile, but the result will not be nearly as smooth in either taste or texture.

Also, the recipe calls for cooking a small amount of beef in water, which creates a mild beef broth with some tender pieces of meat that provide additional taste and texture. If you wish, you can substitute a mild beef broth. For example, add 1 part water to each 1 part uncondensed beef broth, and maybe add a few pieces of previously cooked meat. If you select this option, be sure and adjust the salt you add to take into account the salt in the canned broth.

Tex-Mex Red Chile Enchilada Sauce

The meat and broth:
1 tablespoon cooking oil
3 ounces lean stewing beef cut into 1/4 inch pieces
10 cups water
1-1/4 inch slice onion
1 bay leaf

The sauce:
The reserved meat and broth or substitute 2 1/2 cups plus 1/3
        cup uncondensed beef broth with an equal amount of
        water.
4 medium or 5 small *ancho* chiles, stems, seeds and veins
        removed
5 tablespoons butter
4-1/2 tablespoons flour
1 tablespoon plus 1 teaspoon powdered cumin
4 cloves garlic
2 teaspoons whole oregano
1/2 cup unsalted tomato sauce
1 teaspoon salt or to taste

Heat a large pot (at least 3 quarts) over high heat until it is very hot. Add the cooking oil and as soon as it begins to smoke add the meat all at once. Be very careful because if the oil becomes too hot it will catch fire.

Allow the meat to cook, untouched, for about 20 to 30 seconds, then stir it briefly and leave it to cook an additional 20–30 seconds. Continue cooking the meat, stirring constantly as in stir-frying, until it is browned. This procedure will give you more crust and therefore more flavor than if you stir-fry the meat from the beginning.

Remove the pot from the heat, allow it to cool for about 15 seconds, and add the water. Be careful! When the water hits the hot surface, steam with the potential to burn will be created.

Bring the water to a boil, skim off any scum that rises to the surface, add the onion and bay leaf, turn down the heat, cover the pot, and cook at a bare simmer for 30 minutes. Remove the top from the pot and continue simmering the meat an additional 30 minutes or until it is very tender.

While the meat is simmering, toast the chiles by placing them on a skillet over medium heat for about 20 seconds on each side. The object is to heat the chiles just enough to bring out their flavor but not so much that they scorch.

Rinse the chiles under cold water, remove their stems and seeds and veins, tear them into small pieces and place them in a blender. Cover them with boiling water and allow them to rehydrate for 20 minutes, then pour off and discard the soaking water.

When the meat is tender, strain the broth and reserve 5 2/3 cups of it. If you have less than 5 2/3 cups broth just add enough water to make that amount. Allow it to cool. Please note that if you use hot liquid in a blender it creates steam that can blow off the top, and cause serious burns.

Pour 1 cup of the reserved, cooled broth into the blender with the chiles, being careful not to include any of the meat, and

48

blend for 1 minute at high speed. Add 2 more cups of broth, also without meat, and blend for a few seconds more. Using the fine blade of a food mill or strainer, strain the pureed chiles into a large bowl, and add the remaining 2 2/3 cups of broth and the cooked meat.

Melt the butter in a 3-quart pot over medium heat, add the flour and cook, stirring constantly with a spoon or wire whisk until the flour begins to turn golden, about 2 minutes. Add the cumin and continue cooking, stirring constantly for 30 seconds more. Remove the pot from the heat and pour in about 3/4 cup of the chile puree and broth mixture and stir until it is thickened and smooth. Add another 3/4 cup liquid and again stir until it is thickened. Return the pot to the heat, and continue adding the liquid in small batches until all of it, including the pieces of meat, has been added.

Using a molcajete or mortar and pestle, grind the garlic and oregano into a paste, add it to the pot and then add the tomato sauce and salt. Bring the sauce to a boil, turn down the heat and simmer, stirring fairly often, until it is thickened, about 20 to 30 minutes. It should be the consistency of a very thin milkshake, as it will thicken further when it is baked in the oven over enchiladas.

Makes 3 to 4 cups sauce, enough for 6 to 8 enchilada plates.

GREEN CHILE ENCHILADA SAUCE

The name of this recipe is somewhat deceptive because the majority of the sauce consists of tomatillos, rather than green chiles. That is not true in New Mexico, where almost all green chile sauces are made with their distinctive fresh chiles. One reason for the difference is that Texas does not have a truly distinctive green chile; we rely on the interior Mexican standbys of jalapeños, *serrano*s and *poblano*s.

Tomatillos can be bought canned, but the insipid, tinny taste will make you wish you had fresh ones. They are not difficult to propagate, as I discovered from several volunteer plants near my house, the result of bits of tomatillo spilled from a construction worker's lunch.

Tomatillo sauces have some potential problems and the most common one relates to the tomatillo itself. All tomatillos are tart in taste, but often, instead of being pleasantly tart with fruity overtones, they can be mouth-puckeringly acidic. The usual solution is to add some sugar to the sauce, but while a pinch or two works in a subtle way, enough to completely mask the over-tartness produces a sweet-and-sour disaster.

The real key to mellowing and rounding the flavor of tomatillos is to add chicken broth, then further reduce the sauce. Some cooks use the water in which the tomatillos were first cooked instead of broth, but the latter does a better job. In fact, you can pretty much regulate the tartness of the dish by adding broth, in addition to a pinch or so of sugar.

Another mistake cooks make with this sauce is to not use any oil or other fat. This is fine if it is to be used as a table salsa. But if it is to be served on enchiladas it requires a little fat to help bind it together and keep it from drying out. In the following version, this is accomplished with a small amount of oil and peanut butter. The latter adds nice body and a subtle flavor.

Yet another problem with tomatillos is that after they are cooked their fresh green color turns yucky. To cure that problem, I simply add a few drops of green food coloring. For those who might consider this unthinkable, please remember that most of the tandoori chicken made in Indian restaurants contains red food coloring, and we are only restoring the tomatillos to something approaching their original color.

In terms of heat, the recipe calls for two *serrano* chiles. This produces a fairly mild sauce, so if your taste runs to more heat add one or two more chiles. You can also substitute jalapeños for the *serrano*s. The results, in terms of heat, should be similar, but will depend on the heat of the individual chiles, which can vary greatly.

Hint: If you use canned or salted chicken broth, do not add additional salt until the end of the cooking process.

Green Chile Enchilada Sauce

1 pound tomatillos, husks and stems removed
1/2 cup coarsely chopped white onion
2 *serrano* chiles
1 clove garlic, peeled
1 tablespoon vegetable oil
1/2 teaspoon dried oregano
1/4 teaspoon sugar
1 1/4 cups chicken broth
1 tablespoon creamy peanut butter
Heaping 1/2 teaspoon salt, or to taste, depending on the salti
ness of the broth
3 drops green food coloring, or to taste (optional)

Cover the tomatillos, onion, chiles and garlic with water in a saucepan and bring to a low simmer. Cook until the tomatillos are soft but have not yet fallen apart, 5 to 10 minutes, then strain off and discard the water. Allow the vegetables to cool slightly, and blend them to a smooth puree.

Heat the vegetable oil over medium high heat, add the contents of the blender, bring the puree to a simmer and add the remaining ingredients, except for the salt and food coloring. Continue cooking at a medium simmer until the sauce is thick enough to coat a spoon, about 15 to 20 minutes. Add the salt and food coloring, if using, and remove from the heat.

Makes about 2 cups of sauce, enough for 4 enchilada plates.

LETTUCE AND TOMATO GARNISH

The cool, crisp texture of shredded lettuce and chopped tomato makes a nice contrast to both the stove and chile heat of Tex-Mex combination plates. The addition of a very small amount of tart vinaigrette will add an extra dimension to the entire dish. (I do not add this dressing to the garnish on crispy tacos, because you will undoubtedly be adding a dressing in the form of salsa.)

Lettuce Garnish

1 teaspoon white vinegar
2 teaspoons vegetable oil
1/4 teaspoon dried oregano
1/4 teaspoon salt
2 cups sliced or shredded lettuce
1/2 cup finely chopped tomatoes

To make the dressing, mix together the vinegar, oil, oregano and salt. Place the lettuce and tomatoes in a bowl and toss them with the dressing. Add the "salad" as a garnish to enchilada or combination plates.

MASTER RECIPE FOR ENCHILADAS

This recipe provides instructions for making Tex-Mex style enchiladas. Following the master recipe is a listing of the most popular types and how to adapt the recipe to prepare each one.

Master Recipe for Enchiladas

12 corn tortillas
Cooking oil or spray oil

The filling:
1 1/2 to 2 cups of your choice of mild cheddar cheese, *picadillo*, shredded beef or shredded chicken. When calculating cheese amounts, plan for 1 ounce per enchilada, which includes 3/4 ounce for the filling, and 1/4 ounce each for the garnish.

The sauce:
Your choice of the Tex-Mex red chile sauce, green chile sauce or the ranchero sauce found in the recipe for *huevos rancheros*. Plan to use about 1/2 cup of sauce for each plate of 2 or 3 enchiladas.

The garnish:
1 cup grated mild cheddar cheese, or 2/3 cup grated mild cheddar mixed with 1/3 cup mozzarella and/or provolone.

Preheat the oven to 375 degrees.

To soften the tortillas, either fry them briefly in about an inch of cooking oil, as described in the introduction to enchiladas, or spray or brush both sides of each tortilla with oil. Stack them in a tortilla warmer or wrap in cloth towels and microwave for 30 to 60 seconds at high, or until they are very flexible.

Place about 2 tablespoons of your filling just off center of each tortilla and roll or fold into cylinders.

Cooks note: Whether enchiladas are formed by rolling them into tight cylinders or folded loosely is strictly a personal choice. I suggest you try both methods and pick your favorite. That these methods produce distinctive differences is testimony to the subtleties that make this seemingly simple dish so fascinating.

For the final preparation, either place three of the enchiladas on each of four oven-proof serving plates or place them all, side by side, into a baking dish. Pour the sauce over the enchiladas, top with the cheese garnish (and finely chopped onions, if you wish) and bake for 10 to 15 minutes, or until the cheese has melted and the sauce is beginning to bubble.

The most popular Tex-Mex enchiladas are the following. Please feel free to try your own combinations; someone already has, and they are probably eaten every day.

Cheese Enchiladas

Enchiladas filled with mild cheddar cheese or a combination of cheeses as described above, sauced with red chile sauce and garnished with more cheese and the ever-optional onions.

Beef Enchiladas

Enchiladas filled with *picadillo* or shredded beef, served with red chile sauce, and garnished with cheese and onion, if desired.

Chicken Enchiladas

Enchiladas filled with shredded chicken, sauced with a red chile sauce, garnished with mild cheddar, Monterey Jack, or mozzarella cheese, and onions if you wish.

Green Chile Enchiladas

These enchiladas are often filled with shredded chicken and sometimes either mozzarella or Monterey Jack cheese, sauced with green chile sauce and garnished with mozzarella or Monterrey Jack cheese, sometimes with the addition of a little mild cheddar.

Ranchero Enchiladas

Enchiladas filled with any of the fillings, sauced with ranchero sauce and garnished with mild cheddar, a white cheese or a combination of the two.

TACOS

Thanks to a legion of mom-and-pop Mexican restaurants, fast food joints and drive-ins, not to mention San Antonio's infamous Chile Queens, tacos achieved popularity in Texas decades before they became Mexico's first offering to join the wider food culture in the United States. Certainly our southern neighbor's best known culinary achievement, this versatile dish has as many permutations as there are types of tortillas and ingredients to fill, sauce and garnish them, with new variations being created every day.

The first corn tortilla is thought to have been made shortly after the appearance of the comal—the griddle used to cook tortillas—in about A.D. 500. Undoubtedly tacos evolved shortly thereafter as Mexican Indians began scooping edibles into their new bread. Not only did the tortilla provide nourishment, it also served as the chief eating utensil, perhaps providing one of the origins of our term "flatware." Pun intended.

As with the names of so many other Mexican foods, there is no clear origin of the word taco. Some experts believe it was a Spanish corruption of one or more Nahuatl words describing different types of tortillas such as *ueitlaxcalli* and *quauhtaqualli* that were eventually shortened to *taco.*

In Mexico, tacos are eaten as snacks or light meals, and are often prepared by street vendors using recipes passed down through several generations. Invariably they are accompanied by at least one and sometimes several salsas, and other garnishes such as *pico de gallo,* grated cheese and cream.

Not surprisingly, Mexican-American cooking, especially the Tex-Mex style, includes tacos similar to those found in Mexico. One of these, tacos *al carbón,* is made from char-broiled fajitas or other cuts of beef, poultry or seafood. While in Mexico, tacos al carbón are made with both corn and flour tortillas, in Tex-Mex cooking they are almost always made with the flour variety.

Another version consists of crisp or semi-crisp corn tortillas, that are, in Tex-Mex cooking, usually filled with a *picadillo*, but also sometimes with shredded beef or chicken, as they often are in Mexico.

One taco that is unique to this side of the border and to Tex-Mex cooking is the puffy taco, found primarily in and around San Antonio. While it is difficult to positively identify the inventor of anything related to Mexican food, available information indicates that a relative of the founder of Henry's Puffy Tacos in San Antonio—where they can still be found—was the first to serve them to the public. Instead of cooking flattened masa or tortilla dough on an ungreased griddle to make conventional tortillas, then frying them to make the usual crispy taco shell, the wraps for puffy tacos are formed by frying the raw, flattened dough, which causes it to puff into a crispy inflated shell. Puffy tacos are usually filled with a beef *picadillo* or shredded chicken.

One of the most engaging tacos on this side of the border is found at Chico's Tacos, a small restaurant chain in El Paso. This Tex-Mex home-style offering consists of corn tortillas rolled around a ground beef filling. They are then fried until crisp and served three at a time beneath a mountain of shredded yellow cheese, literally swimming in a thin tomato and chile sauce. Although they are technically *flautas*, we won't quibble with the terminology as these quirky morsels are responsible for long lines at each of the small chain's locations at nearly any hour.

Also popular throughout Texas is the breakfast taco. This welcome contribution to morning dining consists of a fluffy, hot flour tortilla filled with scrambled eggs combined with some or all of the following: fried onion, chiles, fried potatoes, refried beans, cheese, tomato, bacon and chorizo. Although similar concoctions can be found in homes and ranches in Mexico, and more recently in a few cafes, the popularity of these A.M. tacos began in Texas.

The following recipes were selected to provide a peek into the astoundingly diverse world of tacos, and to include terrific versions of some of the most interesting and popular tacos found in Tex-Mex cooking.

MUCH-BETTER-THAN-USUAL TEX-MEX TACOS

These tacos represent by far the most popular style of taco found in Tex-Mex cooking. Two elements combine to make them better than similar versions: the semi-crisp, rather than crisp, corn tortilla shells and the way the *picadillo* (ground beef filling), guacamole, beans and cheese are layered sideways rather than stacked on top of each other.

Much-Better-than-Usual Tex-Mex Tacos

Cooking oil
8 corn tortillas
1 cup refried beans (homemade or canned), heated
1 cup grated, mild cheddar cheese
1 cup guacamole (see recipe index)
1-1/2 cups *picadillo* (see recipe index)
1-1/2 cups shredded lettuce
1 cup tomato, cut into 1/4 inch pieces
Salsa
Heat an oven to 225 degrees.

The taco shells are cooked to a medium crisp, which means they should be crispy but still pliable. It is better for the shells to be underdone rather than overdone, because if they are too crisp they will be difficult to fill and will break at the first bite.

To make them, first heat about 3/4 of an inch of cooking oil in a small-to medium-sized skillet until a tortilla dipped into the oil with kitchen tongs begins to cook vigorously. Lower a tortilla into the hot oil and allow it to cook for a few seconds. If it does not cook vigorously and immediately begin to crisp, increase the heat.

Flip the tortilla over and cook another few seconds. Before it becomes too crisp, grab one edge of the tortilla with the tongs and fold it into a wide v-shape—about one-half of it will be out of the oil—and allow it to crisp a bit more. Then grasp the cooked portion with the tongs, immerse the uncooked portion and continue cooking until it is also semi-crisp, about 15 to 20 seconds for each side. If necessary, place the tongs between the two sides of the tortilla to keep them apart.

Remove the taco shells and drain on absorbent towels. Place them on a plate in the warm oven. Make the remaining shells in the same fashion.

To complete the tacos, spread about 2 tablespoons of beans on one side of each shell, then sprinkle about 2 tablespoons of the cheese onto the beans. Spread about 2 tablespoons of guacamole onto the other side of each shell, then spoon some of the *picadillo* into the middle. Garnish with the lettuce, tomato, any remaining cheese, and serve with the salsa.

Serves 4.

FLOUR TACOS

Flour tacos are simply tacos made with flour tortillas. The most popular versions include: Tacos *al carbón* (tacos filled with char-broiled meat), tacos with *picadillo*, tacos *de carne guisada* (tacos filled with a Tex-Mex beef chile stew), breakfast tacos and tacos with shredded beef or chicken. Another all-time favorite is the basic but delicious taco filled with only refried beans and cheese, a staple of Tex-Mex cooking.

The following tacos are all made in the same manner, with the filling placed inside a hot flour tortilla, topped with salsa or a relish such as *pico de gallo* and/or guacamole, then folded and eaten. Hint: For the best texture, flour tortillas should be heated on an ungreased skillet or griddle. They can also be wrapped in foil and heated in an oven at 350 degrees. A microwave is another option, but if you overheat them they will be unpleasantly tough.

TACOS AL CARBÓN

In both Mexico and the United States, tacos *al carbón* are made from different cuts of meat, poultry and fish. Most often they are made with beef, in Texas most often from fajitas (skirt steak) (see recipe index) or with *agujas* (see recipe index) or another part of the chuck. Also popular are tacos *al carbón* prepared with fajita-style chicken (see recipe index). The traditional garnishes include guacamole, *pico de gallo* and a salsa.

Tacos al Carbón

8 flour tortillas
1-1/2 pounds chopped char-broiled, beef, such as fajitas,
     chuck steak, chicken, shrimp or fish
Pico de gallo (see recipe index)
Guacamole (see recipe index)
Salsa

To make the tacos, heat the tortillas, fill them with the beef or chicken, then garnish them with the pico de gallo, guacamole and salsa.

Tacos de Picadillo
(Tacos with ground a meat filling)

8 flour tortillas
1 1/2 cups *picadillo* (see recipe index)

Pico de gallo (see recipe index)
Guacamole (see recipe index)
1 1/2 cups shredded lettuce
1 cup shredded mild cheddar cheese
Salsa

To fill the tacos, heat the *picadillo* and place about 3 table-spoons inside each tortilla. Top with *pico de gallo,* guacamole, shredded lettuce, some of the cheese and salsa.
Serves 4.

Tacos de Carne guisada

8 flour tortillas
Carne Guisada (see recipe index)

To make the tacos, heat the tortillas and spoon the stew into them.

Flour Tacos with Shredded Beef or Chicken

8 flour tortillas
1-1/2 cups shredded beef or chicken filling (see recipe index)
1-1/2 cups shredded lettuce
1 cup shredded, mild cheddar cheese
1 cup guacamole (see recipe index)
1 cup refried beans (see recipe index) (optional)
Salsa

Heat the tortillas, fill them with the beef or chicken, then gar-nish them with the lettuce, cheese, guacamole and beans (if using them). Serve with the salsa.

BREAKFAST TACOS

Breakfast tacos are usually made by combining scrambled eggs with just about every imaginable breakfast food from bacon to hash-brown potatoes, then wrapping them in a flour tortilla and serving with a favorite salsa.

Tex-Mex breakfast tacos often include some canned *Rotel* brand tomatoes and chiles. This is a particularly easy way to prepare them, especially when cooking for a crowd. However, if you want a very special breakfast taco, combine a few of the ingredients, such as cooked *chorizo* and onions and make a 1-egg omelet in a 5-inch skillet, place it on a flour tortilla, then top with whatever other items you prefer before folding. The extra time and effort will be repaid with a much more interesting taco. Following are recipes for both types.

Typical Breakfast Tacos

2 tablespoons cooking oil
8 ounces *chorizo* (about 3/4 cup)
4 slices bacon, finely chopped
1 pound potatoes, peeled and cut into 1/4 inch dice (about 3
    cups)
8 large eggs
1/2 cup well-drained, chopped, canned Rotel brand toma-

toes, or substitute another brand of chopped tomatoes and add 2
jalapeño chiles, stemmed, seeded and peeled

    1/2 cup loosely packed, chopped cilantro

    1 teaspoon dried oregano

    1/2 teaspoon salt

    1/2 teaspoon black pepper

    1/4 pound grated mozzarella cheese (about 1 cup tightly
        packed)

    1/4 pound grated mild cheddar cheese (about 1 cup tightly
        packed)

    12 flour tortillas

    2 tablespoons butter

    3/4 cup refried beans, heated (optional)

    Salsa

Heat a skillet over medium heat, add the cooking oil, *chorizo*
and bacon. Cook, stirring frequently, until the chorizo and bacon
are just cooked through, add the potatoes and continue cooking
until the potatoes are tender and beginning to brown.

Meanwhile, beat the eggs in a large bowl and add the Rotel
tomatoes (or regular tomatoes and jalapeños), cilantro, oregano,
salt, pepper and cheeses, and reserve them.

When the potatoes are nearly done, heat the tortillas on an
ungreased skillet over medium heat until very hot and beginning
to brown on one side, and reserve them. When the potatoes are
done, add the butter to them, and when it has melted pour the egg
mixture over them. Scramble the ingredients until the eggs are as
firm as you like.

To prepare the tacos, if you are including refried beans spread
a very thin layer of them onto each tortilla, spoon some of the
scrambled egg mixture over the beans, and serve with your
favorite salsa.

Makes 12 tacos.

Special Breakfast Tacos

1/2 tablespoon vegetable oil
2 jalapeño chiles, stemmed seeded and finely chopped
1/4 cup *chorizo*
2 tablespoons finely chopped cilantro
4 eggs
2 tablespoons butter
4 slices provolone cheese
3/4 cup hash brown potatoes
4 hot flour tortillas
3/4 cup refried beans

Heat the vegetable oil in a skillet over medium heat, add the chiles and *chorizo* and fry, breaking up the chorizo as much as possible with the edge of a spoon until it is cooked through and becoming crisp. Then stir in the cilantro and allow to cool.

Crack open each egg into a small bowl. Add equal portions of the cooled chorizo mixture into each egg and beat. Heat a 5-inch skillet, preferably with a non-stick surface, over medium heat, add and swirl around 1/2 tablespoon of the butter as it melts. When the butter begins to brown pour in the contents of one of the bowls, swirl it to cover the entire bottom of the pan, then continue to cook until the eggs are well set, but still a little runny.

Place a slice of provolone in the center of the omelette, then top with some fried potatoes. Spread a thin layer of refried beans on one of the hot tortillas. Then, using a spatula, place the small omelet onto the tortilla, add salsa to taste and fold into a taco. Repeat the process for the remaining tacos.

Serves 4.

BEAN-AND-CHEESE FLOUR TACOS

This is the standby dish for Tex-Mex aficionados on a budget. They are made many different ways, but this one, perhaps more technically a *quesadilla* than a taco, is my favorite. The quality of the taco will depend on the quality of the ingredients. So while it can be made with canned refried beans and supermarket flour tortillas, it will be night-and day-better if those items are made from scratch.

Unlike other flour tacos, there is nothing crunchy enough in the filling to give the taco texture. For that reason the recipe calls for them to be heated with a little butter until the outside of the tortillas is a crisp golden brown.

Bean-and-Cheese Tacos

4 ounces grated, mild cheddar cheese
4 ounces grated, smoked provolone cheese
8 flour tortillas
2 cups refried beans
1/2 cup minced, pickled jalapeño chiles
1/2 cup of your favorite salsa
1/4 cup melted butter

Mix the two cheeses together. Heat the tortillas on an ungreased skillet over medium heat and wrap them in a towel. Leave the skillet on the heat, then in another pan or in a microwave heat the beans until they are quite warm, but not boiling hot.

Place the warmed tortillas on a work surface and spread 1/4 cup of the beans on one-half of each tortilla. Cover the beans on each tortilla with 1 ounce (1/8 of the total) of the mixed cheeses, sprinkle on a tablespoon of the jalapeños, and about 1 tablespoon of the salsa. Fold the uncovered half of each tortilla over to make turnovers, and press them lightly together.

Coat the skillet over medium heat with just enough of the butter to make a thin film and place the folded tacos onto it. Cook the tacos until the bottoms are golden brown, turn them and do the same on the other side, adding a little more butter if necessary. You will probably have to do this in two batches.

Makes 8 tacos.

PUFFY TACOS AND TOSTADAS

Puffy tacos are a Tex-Mex original. All the evidence suggests they were first sold to the public in San Antonio. Surprisingly, they are seldom found elsewhere.

Instead of being made with corn tortillas, puffy tacos are made by forming and frying the tortilla dough into crisp, puffy little pillows, then filled. Two elements combine to make cooking puffy tacos a bit tricky: The oil must be at the proper temperature, and, in order to avoid breaking them, the shells must be formed with a dexterity that requires a little practice.

Fortunately, the techniques are quickly learned, and the latter problem is easily solved if you decide that, rather than making puffy tacos requiring V-shaped shells, you would rather make puffy tostadas, which are served flat.

Puffy Tacos

The taco shells:
Dough made from 2 cups MaSeca or Masa Harina (corn
    flour for making corn tortillas)
Cooking oil
A tortilla press
Wax paper

Make the dough following the directions on the package and divide it into 12 separate balls. This will make enough for 12 shells and allow for some mistakes, since you will only need 8 shells for the recipe.

To form the dough, put a piece of wax paper (you can also use plastic wrap or pieces cut from plastic garbage bags) a little larger than your tortilla press on the bottom of the press. Place a round of dough onto the plastic just off center toward the hinges, then cover it with another piece of wax paper. Close the press firmly to make a thin circle about 4 to 5 inches in diameter.

To fry the shells, heat about 2 inches of cooking oil in a pot over medium heat to 350 degrees. Remove the wax paper-covered, formed dough from the press. The potentially dangerous part of the process is getting the dough into the hot oil without burning yourself.

This is how the pros do it: Peel off the top layer of wax paper or plastic and invert the formed dough, with the exposed side down, on top of the palm of your right hand (if you are right-handed) and peel off the remaining piece of wax paper or plastic. Pass the hand with the dough over the oil and, using an upward sweeping motion, release the dough into the hot oil, being careful not to burn yourself.

A much safer way is to place the exposed dough on top of a large, flat Teflon spatula instead of on your hand, then remove the top layer of wax paper or plastic and lower the spatula into the oil. In either case the dough should begin to puff immediately. If it does not, increase the heat.

Using the spatula or a large cooking spoon, spoon some oil over the top of the dough. It will quickly puff and begin to turn golden. Again, using the side of the spatula or spoon, press down on the center of the tortilla to form an indentation to hold the filling, or leave them flat if you are making puffy tostadas. Continue cooking a few more seconds until the shell is golden brown and crispy.

Alternatively, you can use cooking tongs to produce the indentation and partially fold the shells while they are cooking, but be careful as they break easily.

The tacos or tostadas:
8 puffy taco or tostada shells
1 1/2 cups ground beef *picadillo* (see recipe index)
1 cup guacamole (see recipe index)
1 cup grated mild cheddar cheese
1-1/2 cups shredded lettuce
1 cup finely chopped tomato
Salsas

Spoon some *picadillo* into each shell, or into the top of each shell if you chose to make puffy tostadas. Top with a little guacamole, grated cheese, lettuce, tomato, and salsa.

Makes 8 tacos.

FLAUTAS

In Mexico, where tacos are almost always either served with hot, unfried corn tortillas or with tortillas that have been only lightly fried, *flautas* are what people turn to for something really crunchy. They consist of corn tortillas wrapped tightly around a filling of shredded beef, pork or chicken, secured with toothpicks, then fried until crispy. Often they are served with a garnish of guacamole and grated *queso cotija*, Mexico's answer to Parmesan cheese, on top. They are easy to make because they can be rolled well before cooking and because, although they are deep-fried, the process requires only about 1 inch of cooking oil.

In Tex-Mex cooking, *flautas* are made the same way, except that *picadillo* is the most common filling, and mild cheddar cheese, rather than *queso cotija*, is used in the garnish.

Preparing the flautas for cooking:

In Mexico, warm, fresh tortillas are wrapped around the filling. In this country our tortillas are much drier, so they tend to crack when rolled. To solve this problem we soften the tortillas in a little hot oil or in the microwave after coating them with a spray of oil, just as we would for enchiladas, before rolling them.

After the tortillas have been softened, place a tablespoon of the filling—or perhaps a little more—in a line across each tortilla, then roll the tortilla snugly around the filling, securing it with a toothpick to keep it from unrolling.

The following recipe serves for *flautas* filled with *picadillo*, shredded beef or chicken or cooked *chorizo* and potato. While these are the most popular Tex-Mex fillings, feel free to make your *flautas* with whatever filling you would like.

Following this all-purpose recipe is one for Chico's-style tacos, a dish very close to the one that has led to fame and presumably fortune for a restaurant chain in El Paso.

Flautas

8 corn tortillas, softened (see above)
3/4 cup filling: *picadillo,* shredded beef, shredded chicken or
   chorizo and potato (see recipe index)
8 toothpicks
Oil for frying
2 cups shredded lettuce mixed with 1/2 cup chopped tomato
1 cup guacamole
1 cup shredded, mild cheddar cheese

Place a softened corn tortilla flat on the work surface. Place slightly more than 1 tablespoon of the filling near the center, and roll the tortilla tightly around it. Secure the uncooked flauta with a toothpick. At this point they can be refrigerated for several hours before being cooked.

Just before serving, heat about 1 inch of cooking oil in a skillet over medium heat until it is hot but not smoking. Using kitchen tongs, immerse an uncooked flauta in the oil and cook until most of it is a crispy, golden brown. If the flauta does not immediately begin to cook vigorously, increase the heat.

With the tongs, turn the *flauta* and continue cooking until it is golden brown all over. Remove the flauta to drain on absorbent towels. Prepare the remaining *flautas* in the same manner. Serve the *flautas,* two per person, topped with some shredded lettuce and chopped tomato, a dollop of guacamole and a sprinkling of the cheese.

Makes 8 flautas.

CHICO'S-STYLE TACOS

Chico's is a small chain of Mexican fast food restaurants in El Paso. Although many of their dishes are popular, it is their tacos that keep them full at all hours of the day and night. This recipe is in the section on *flautas* because that is technically what they are.

Chico's did not provide this recipe, but it is close enough to the original that a transplanted El Pasoan declared it to be a complete cure for the withdrawal symptoms she had experienced since moving to Colorado. It is a wonderful example of Tex-Mex home-style cooking adapted to restaurant service, in that the sauces and filling are all part of a one-pot cooking process.

Chico's-Style Tacos

The filling and the broth:
3/4 pound ground beef (15%–20% fat)
4 1/2 cups water
Heaping 1/2 teaspoon salt, or to taste
3 large or 4 small jalapeños, stems removed
1/4 cup canned, crushed tomato

Place the ground beef in a medium-sized pot, add 2/3 cup of the water and stir to break up the meat. Bring the mixture nearly to a simmer, continuing to stir, then add the remaining water. Bring the mixture to a simmer, then skim off and discard any scum that rises to the surface.

Turn down the heat, add the salt and jalapeños and simmer, covered, for 20 minutes, or until the jalapeños are soft. Pour the contents of the pot through a strainer set over a bowl large enough to contain the liquid. (There will be 4 to 4 1/2 cups). Reserve the meat and chiles. Bring the strained broth to a simmer,

add the crushed tomato and simmer for 2 to 3 minutes, then turn
the heat to very low.

The Sauce:
The reserved jalapeños
3/4 cup water
1/2 teaspoon salt, or to taste

When the jalapeños are cool enough to handle, slice off the
stem end and, if you wish, remove some or all of the veins and
seeds. Removing the veins makes the sauce a little milder. While
removing the seeds does not affect the heat, it does eliminate their
unpleasant texture and slightly bitter flavor.

Place the chiles in a blender, add the water and salt and blend
until pureed. Reserve.

The Tacos:
12 small, thin corn tortillas
The reserved filling
12 toothpicks
Cooking oil
The reserved broth
8 ounces (about 3 1/2 to 4 very loosely packed cups) finely
    grated, mild cheddar cheese
The reserved sauce

If the tortillas are very fresh and soft, you can roll them tightly without causing them to crack or unroll. If not, you will need
to soften them. This can be done by quickly passing them through
the hot oil before you fry the tacos and draining them on paper
towels. An easier and less messy method is to spray them with a
little spray-oil on both sides, wrap them in a towel, or place them

in a plastic tortilla warmer and microwave them for about 30 seconds, or until they are very pliable.

In either case, place 1 1/2 to 2 tablespoons of the filling just off center of each tortilla, roll them into tight cylinders, secure them in the middle with a toothpick and reserve them.

To fry the tacos, pour cooking oil into a small- or medium-sized skillet to a depth of about 1 inch. Heat it over medium- to medium-high heat until very hot but not smoking. Using kitchen tongs, place the tacos in the oil and fry, turning them once, until they are crisp and golden brown. Remove the tacos from the oil and drain on absorbent towels.

To serve, place the tacos (3 each is the usual serving) in large, shallow soup bowls, ladle some of the broth over them to whatever depth you prefer. (Chico's covers them.) Top with the cheese and serve with the sauce. Aficionados mix the sauce into the broth, covering the tacos.

Makes 12 tacos.

TAMALES

While there are probably more than a thousand different tamales in Mexico, only one type is commonly served in Tex-Mex restaurants. It is relatively small and features a fragrant pork and red chile filling. Not surprisingly, its origins are in northern Mexico, across the border from Texas, and in particular in the state of Nuevo León.

Until recently it was difficult for many in the United Stated to make really great tamales at home because not everyone had access to the proper *masa,* which is similar to that used to make corn tortillas but with a coarser grind. Home cooks usually either bought the *masa* prepared for tortillas from tortilla factories or made it with the *Masa* Harina or MaSeca corn flour for tortillas sold in grocery stores. Sometimes they would combine ordinary cornmeal with mashed, canned hominy.

Now, however, MaSeca sells a more coarsely ground corn flour especially formulated for tamales that is widely distributed throughout the southwest, and that does an excellent job. If you cannot find it you will have to substitute the more easily found MaSeca or *Masa* Harina corn flour for tortillas, which will do a satisfactory job. Be careful, as the MaSeca packages for corn tortillas and tamales are similar. The Maseca package of all-purpose corn flour that is really best suited to tortillas and gorditas is labeled Instant Corn *Masa* Mix for corn tortillas, tamales, enchiladas . . . . The mix that is, by far, the best for tamales is simply called Instant Corn *Masa* Mix for Delicious Tamales.

Spaniards introduced fat, usually in the form of lard, to Mexico and to the previously dry and rather uninteresting tamales made by the Indians, transforming them into something special. Lard is really the only fat that should be used to make traditional tamales, as nothing properly imitates its flavor. For those concerned about fat, remember that good lard actually has less saturated fat than butter.

However, a major problem in this regard is that most supermarket lard also contains partially hydrogenated fat and has a yucky flavor. If you cannot find pure lard at Hispanic groceries you can make it yourself, using the recipe in the section for flour tortillas.

The best substitute in terms of texture is shortening, which has large quantities of partially hydrogenated fat that nutrition experts believe to be more harmful to health than saturated fat.

The most important elements involved in making tamales are to properly measure the lard, *masa* and broth, to beat the fat until creamy, then to beat it with the *masa* and liquid until it is light and fluffy. Because measuring by volume can be both imprecise and messy, especially regarding the fat, it is advisable to use an electronic kitchen scale. Good models are available for around $50.

The beating can be done by hand or with a hand mixer, but by far the easiest method is to use a stand mixer. This piece of equipment is specified in the recipe. If you wish to make tamales with a hand mixer or completely by hand, simply continue beating until the described results are obtained.

After making the dough and filling, the tamales must be formed and wrapped. To make perfect tamales takes both skill and patience. Fortunately, producing decent tamales takes much less of each. Most tamales are wrapped in corn husks, but parchment paper or even white cotton sheeting can be used.

Dried husks in Mexico are usually sold whole, which means that instead of being flat, they have a nice, rounded shape at one end that holds the *masa* and keeps it from escaping during cooking, and they taper to a point at the other. In the United States commercially-available husks are usually cut by machine, which means that they are flat, with a straight-cut flat end and a tapered end, which requires an extra step in the process of assembling the tamales.

Once the tamales have been formed they should be steamed as soon as possible. Special *tamaleras* are sold in Hispanic groceries for the purpose, but are unnecessary, particularly for the relatively small quantity of tamales called for in the recipe. You can use a collapsible vegetable steamer fitted into a pot or any device that is perforated to allow steam to reach the tamales and that can be placed at least 2 inches above the 3 to 5 inches of water called for in the recipe. A fryer basket placed upside down in a large pot works well to support the steamer.

The most important considerations are to keep the simmering water from actually touching the tamales and to have a tight-fitting lid that keeps as much of the steam as possible from escaping.

Tex-Mex Tamales

First prepare the filling, which can be done several days before you make the tamales, and ideally requires at least 3 hours of rest in the refrigerator. Just remember to save the 3 tablespoons chile sauce to put into the dough. Also, if you use canned, salted chicken broth to make the *masa*, remember to adjust the quantity of salt accordingly.

The filling:
2 tablespoons vegetable oil
3/4 pound boneless pork, cut into 1/3 inch pieces
4 cups water
2 *ancho* chiles, stemmed and seeded
3/4 teaspoon powdered cumin
1 teaspoon oregano
2 cloves garlic
1/4 teaspoon black pepper
1 teaspoon salt, or to taste

Heat the oil in a large pot over medium high to high heat, add the pork and cook, stirring often until it is just browned. Add 4 cups water, bring to a boil and simmer, covered, for about 40 minutes, or until the pork is very tender. Remove the pot from the heat and reserve, separately, both the cooking liquid and the pork.

Cover the chiles with hot water and allow them to soak for 20 minutes. Discard the soaking water and place the chiles in a blender with the cumin, oregano, garlic, pepper, salt and 1/2 cup of reserved pork broth. Blend the mixture for 1 minute, add an additional 1 1/4 cups pork broth and blend another minute. (If you do not have enough broth, simply add water.)

Remove 3 tablespoons of this chile sauce to use later in the *masa*, and pour the rest of the sauce over the reserved pork in a saucepan. Simmer the sauce and pork until the sauce is very thick, about 10 to 15 minutes. If you have the time, refrigerate the pork mixture for at least 3 hours, or up to three days.

The masa:
1 3/4 cups MaSeca Instant Corn Masa Mix for Delicious
   Tamales (see above)—about 9 ounces
1 1/2 cups plus 1 tablespoon chicken broth or water
3 tablespoons reserved chile sauce
1 teaspoon baking powder
1 teaspoon salt (or less, if using canned chicken broth)
10 tablespoons lard at room temperature—about 5 ounces
   (see index for information on lard)

Place the dry corn flour in a bowl, add the broth or water and reserved chile sauce. Mix with a wooden spoon, then knead briefly with your hands to make sure all the liquid is incorporated. Cover the bowl with plastic wrap or a damp towel and allow the corn flour to re-hydrate for 30 minutes.

Place the fat in the bowl of a stand mixer. Beat it at medium to medium-high speed until it is light and creamy, scraping down the bowl as necessary, about 2 minutes. Add the baking powder and salt and beat for another minute. Add the re-hydrated *masa* and, beginning at low speed and gradually increasing to medium high, beat for 1 minute. Continue beating for 10 minutes at medium high, stopping to scrape down the sides of the bowl 2 or 3 times, or as necessary.

77

Test the *masa* by taking a 1/2-inch piece and placing it carefully in a glass of cold water, where it should float. If it does not, continue beating for another 2 minutes. If it still does not float the measurements are probably off and a little more room temperature fat should be added, a tablespoon at a time, until the dough floats.

The tamales:
12 dried corn husks
The filling
The *masa*
Kitchen string or strips torn from additional corn husks to tie
    the tamales
A steamer

Before using the dried husks you must first re-hydrate them to make them pliable. To do this, place them in a large pot or bowl, cover them with hot water, and allow them to soak for at least 2 hours. You may have to place something heavy on them to keep them submerged.

When they are pliable, remove them from the water and towel off the excess moisture. Spread about 3 to 4 tablespoons of the *masa* into a square of about 3 1/2 to 4 inches, beginning about 2 inches down from the flat end of the husks and about an inch from the left side. Place about 1 1/2 to 2 tablespoons of the filling down the center of the *masa*, then fold the sides over it and roll into a cylinder. Twist the flat top end together and tie it with either kitchen twine or a strip of corn husk, just above the *masa*, then either twist and tie the other end, or fold it up and over the joint and tie it around the circumference of the tamale.

To steam the tamales, bring 3 to 5 inches of water to a boil in the bottom of a steamer, place the tamales in a perforated container lined with a layer of husks, well above the water, cover and steam at medium-high heat for about 1 hour. Some cooks add a small coin to the steaming liquid, as the noise of its bouncing around the pot will warn them if all the water evaporates. Turn off the heat and allow the tamales to remain covered for 15 minutes. Remove the cover and open one of the tamales. If it does not stick to the husk they are done. If it sticks, steam an additional 10 to 15 minutes.

The recipe makes about 12 tamales of 1/4 cup masa each, and quantities can be increased proportionately.

QUESADILLAS

Quesadillas are made by sandwiching cheese and other filling ingredients between tortillas, then heating them until the outside begins to crisp and the cheese melts. They are one of the easiest and most versatile offerings in Mexican cooking.

As the name implies, their main ingredient is cheese, but that is about the only constant, as they are made in different ways with different additional ingredients in different parts of Mexico and the United States. In Mexico they are most often made with corn tortillas and cheese, either by folding the tortilla turnover-style over a cheese filling or sandwiching cheese between two tortillas and frying the result on both sides in very little oil.

In either case the *quesadilla* is cooked until it begins to turn golden on the outsides, but the tortilla remains fairly soft. If made turnover-style, the *quesadilla* is usually served whole. If made sandwich-style, it is sliced like a pizza into wedges.

In some parts of Mexico, *quesadilla*s are made by enclosing the filling in uncooked tortilla dough and frying them until crisp. The result resembles tiny, crisp *empanadas.* In addition to the cheese, *quesadilla* fillings include items such as squash blossoms, *huitlacoche* (corn mushrooms) chiles, *chorizo, picadillo,* fajitas and just about anything else that might appeal.

In Tex-Mex cooking, *quesadilla*s are basically a Mexican version of the grilled-cheese sandwich. They are made with both corn and flour tortillas, with flour probably being the most common and easiest to prepare. In most restaurants they go far beyond the simple cheese variety, with *picadillo*, fajitas, chicken-fajita-style, and chorizo being favorite additions. Besides the cheese and meats, some *pico de gallo* and/or table salsa is also often included.

These Tex-Mex *quesadilla*s are quick and easy to fix, make great appetizers and party-fare and are also ideal for a light lunch or dinner. They are also perfect vehicles for expressing your own creativity.

The following includes a basic *quesadilla* recipe that provides instruction for both turnover and flat, sandwich-style *quesadillas*, then offers suggestions for more elaborate combinations. Please note that while flour tortillas are specified, these *quesadillas* can also be made with corn tortillas. *Quesadillas* are delicious topped with guacamole.

Quesadillas, Plain and Fancy

This is the most basic quesadilla found in Tex-Mex cooking.

Butter or cooking oil
8 flour tortillas
2 cups grated, mild cheddar, mozzarella, Monterey Jack, or a
    combination of cheeses
1/2 cup sliced, pickled jalapeños, or to taste

To make turnover-style *quesadillas*, heat enough butter or oil over medium heat to lightly coat a large skillet. Place a tortilla onto the skillet and sprinkle 1/4 cup cheese over half of it. Sprinkle on some jalapeños, then fold the uncovered half of the tortilla over the filling and hold it in place with the flat side of a spatula.

Continue heating until the bottom of the folded *quesadilla* is a light golden-brown and the cheese is beginning to melt, adjusting the heat as necessary. With the spatula, turn the *quesadilla* and continue cooking it on the other side until it is golden-brown and all the cheese has melted. Prepare the remaining *quesadillas* in the same manner.

To make sandwich-style *quesadillas*, you also begin by placing a tortilla on the lightly greased skillet. You then sprinkle twice the amount of cheese and jalapeños over its entire surface, and top it with a second tortilla.

Brush the top of the second tortilla with a little oil or melted butter and continue cooking until the cheese begins to melt and the bottom of the bottom tortilla is beginning to turn golden. Using a large spatula, flip the *quesadilla* over and cook on the other side until the bottom is golden-brown and the cheese is completely melted.

Makes 8 turnover-style or 4 sandwich-style quesadillas.

More Elaborate Quesadillas

To make more elaborate *quesadillas*, simply add your choices from the list below—or from your own imagination—to the above recipe before folding the tortilla or topping it with a second one. If you wish, serve the *quesadillas* with guacamole, and your favorite salsa.

Optional fillings:
Pico de gallo (see recipe index)
Picadillo (see recipe index)
Fried, crumbled Mexican chorizo and sliced avocado
Fajitas (see recipe index)
Chicken, fajita-style (see recipe index)
Refried beans (see recipe index)
Shredded beef (see recipe index)
Shredded chicken (see recipe index)
Shredded or chopped country-style spare ribs (see recipe index)
Cooked spinach or other vegetables, for a vegetarian *que sadilla*

CHILES RELLENOS

Tex-Mex chiles rellenos are usually made with the same *poblano* chiles as those in Mexico's interior, although some cooks occasionally use the thinner, longer Anaheim chile. They are then filled, dipped in batter, and fried.

The first step in the process is to remove the skins from the chiles. To do this they must be blistered. This is best done over a strong gas flame or the flame from a newly kindled wood fire, scorching the chiles until their skins are blackened. It can also be effectively accomplished by immersing the chiles in a deep fat fryer, with the oil heated to 350 degrees, until the skins turn into white blisters.

The more intense the heat the quicker the chile's skin will be roasted and the less the chile will be cooked. This is important because the more cooked through the chile, the limper and more liable it will be to fall apart. A still-firm chile is ideal.

I often roast *poblano* chiles for other uses under an oven broiler or in an electric toaster oven. This method will work for stuffing chiles, but, because of the lower heat, more skill will be required to keep the whole thing from falling apart. A great time to roast chiles is just after starting a mesquite cooking fire, before the wood burns to coals. Whatever method is used to burn the chiles' skins, after this is accomplished the chiles should be placed in plastic bags to sweat for about 20 minutes, which makes the skins much easier to remove.

After the skins have been removed (some cooks refuse to rinse the chiles during the process because it eliminates some of the smoke or roasted flavor) they should be carefully slit down one side and cleaned of all seeds and prominent veins, leaving them as intact as possible with the stem in place. They can then be stuffed with either cheese or *picadillo*—or both—and set aside until the batter is made and the oil heated.

As with so many other aspects of Tex-Mex cooking, chiles rellenos are usually filled with less complex *picadillo*s and different cheeses than their south-of-the-border counterparts.

The traditional batter for *chiles rellenos* consists of egg whites beaten with a little salt to stiff peaks, then folded into an equal number of lightly beaten egg yolks. Some cooks add just a little flour to the eggs to help bind the mixture. Some dust the outside of the chiles with flour to help the batter adhere.

The chiles are fried in about 3/4 inch of vegetable oil heated to about 350 degrees in a skillet. Since it is difficult to use a thermometer in such shallow oil, I heat the oil until a drop of water placed in the oil immediately vaporizes. This method works well—but be careful, as any more than a tiny drop of water can cause the oil to spatter and cause burns. A skillet rather than a high-sided pot is used so that you can get a spatula underneath the frying chiles at an angle low enough to turn and remove them. While coating the chiles and getting them into the oil takes a bit of practice, any unbattered areas can be easily fixed by spooning additional batter over them.

Chiles rellenos are traditionally served on top of a thin, mildly-hot tomato sauce. Most restaurants use one made with canned tomato puree. You can do this, but if you are willing to take a little extra time preparing fresh tomatoes the flavor will be far better.

Tex-Mex Chiles Rellenos

8 *poblano* chiles, skins removed, but left whole with the stem
    intact (see above)
8 chunks of mozzarella cheese cut to fit the inside of your
    chiles, about 3 inches long by 2 inches wide by 1/4 inch
    thick, or 2 cups *picadillo* (see recipe index)
Flour for dusting the chiles
4 eggs, separated
1/2 teaspoon salt
Vegetable oil

Tuck a piece of cheese into each skinned chile, or spoon 3 to
4 tablespoons *picadillo* inside each of them. Or you can do as
some cooks do, and stuff the chiles with both cheese and *picadillo*, using approximately half the normal amount for each one. The
fillings should be completely enclosed. Dust the outside of the
chiles with just a little flour. A fine strainer or flour sifter works
well for this. Set the chiles aside while you make the batter.

To prepare the batter, add the salt to the egg whites and beat
them to stiff peaks. Beat the yolks until creamy and carefully fold
the whites into them. The batter should be used immediately, as it
will quickly separate.

Heat about 3/4 of an inch of vegetable oil in a skillet over
medium to medium-high heat until a drop of water instantly
vaporizes, being careful not to add more than a tiny drop as per
the warning above.

Holding a chile by the stem and supporting it with a spatula
or large, slotted kitchen spoon, immerse it into the batter, then
carefully lower it into the hot oil, making sure to keep your fingers
well out of the way of any spatters, which can cause serious burns.
Allow the chile to fry until it is well browned on the bottom.

Using the spatula or slotted spoon, and kitchen tongs, carefully turn the chile, and fry until golden-brown on the other side. You can repair any problems by spooning additional batter onto the chile and frying it. Remove the chile to absorbent towels to drain.

To serve, spoon some sauce onto serving plates and top with the fried chiles. They can be prepared several hours ahead, refrigerated, and then reheated in a 350-degree oven until they are hot and the cheese melted.

Serves 4 to 8.

The sauce:
3 medium-sized tomatoes
1 or 2 jalapeño chiles, stemmed, seeded and cut in half
1/2 teaspoon salt, or to taste
1 tablespoon olive oil

Place the tomatoes and jalapeños in a large pot, cover them with water and bring to a boil. Simmer the tomatoes until they are soft, about 3 to 5 minutes. Remove the tomatoes and chiles from the water and allow them to cool. Remove the skins from the tomatoes and place them and the chiles in a blender. Add the salt and blend to a smooth puree.

Heat a saucepan over medium heat, add the oil, then add the blended tomato and chiles. Simmer, stirring frequently, until the sauce thickens just enough to coat the back of a spoon.

Makes 8 chiles rellenos.

GORDITAS

Gorditas means "little fat ones," a good description of this classic *antojito*. They can be served as appetizers, topped with nothing but a dollop of guacamole and a sprinkling of cheese, or as an entree item, for which they are usually slit nearly in half and filled with a *picadillo* or other filling to make taco-like sandwiches. In Mexico, entire fast food operations offering a large selection of fillings are devoted to *gorditas*. In Tex-Mex restaurants they are usually offered either as a combination plate alternative or a la carte.

Most *gorditas* are made with the *masa* or dough for tortillas to which a small amount of lard has been added. The dough is then patted into small circles about 1/4 inch thick. The formed dough is then cooked in a two-part process: toasted on a griddle until cooked through, then fried in a small amount of lard or oil to make them crispy.

However, since this book is about "the best" and not "the usual," the following recipe is for gorditas with a special twist. They are the best I have ever had.

One of the most interesting restaurants in Nuevo Laredo, across the border from Laredo, Texas is called El Rincón del Viejo, "The Old Man's Corner." It is well away from the tourist center and somewhat difficult to find, but it is a pantheon to Northern Mexico cooking that is frequented by in-the-know people from all over South Texas.

What makes their signature *gorditas* special is the addition of mashed potatoes to the usual corn *masa*. They serve their gorditas as appetizers and cook them only on the lightly greased griddle. I adapted the following recipe from the original, and present it with two options: smaller appetizer *gorditas* cooked just once and the larger, filled version that is fried after the initial griddle cooking. While these versions are admittedly not traditional, I think they are the best!

Northern Mexican Potato Gorditas

For an appetizer these can be made small, cooked on a griddle and served with guacamole and other toppings, or they can be made larger, fried in oil after being cooked on the griddle and served with the filling in the middle, taco-style. Although shortening or vegetable oil can be substituted for the lard, much of the authentic flavor will be lost.

For the gorditas:

14 ounces *masa* for corn tortillas, either from MasSeca or fresh ground (approximately 1 1/2 cups dry mix plus 3/4 cup plus 3 tablespoons water)

9 ounces mashed, boiled potato, weighed after peeling (approximately 1 3/4 cups chopped potato) and before cooking

2 teaspoons melted lard.

Additional lard

Cooking oil

Optional toppings and fillings:

Guacamole

Mexican *quesa fresco,* Monterey Jack or goat cheese

Picadillo or one of the shredded meat fillings.

To make either style of *gorditas,* mix together the tortilla *masa,* mashed potato and 2 teaspoons melted lard.

To make thin, appetizer *gorditas,* pat small pieces of the dough into circles about 2 1/2 inches in diameter and between 1/8 and 1/4 inch thick. Heat a skillet over medium heat, add enough lard to just film the surface and cook the dough until it begins to turn golden on both sides and is cooked through. Put guacamole or other toppings on them and serve immediately.

To make larger *gorditas,* pat larger pieces of the dough into circles about 3 inches in diameter and about 1/4 inch thick and cook in the lard-filmed skillet as above. When they are done, fry the gorditas in about 1/2 inch cooking oil, heated over medium heat until a drop of water sputters immediately, about 350 degrees. Drain the cooked gorditas. When they are cool enough to handle, slit them almost—but not entirely—in half lengthwise and fill them with your favorite filling, such as *picadillo* or shredded meat. Garnish them with guacamole, salsa and pico de gallo.

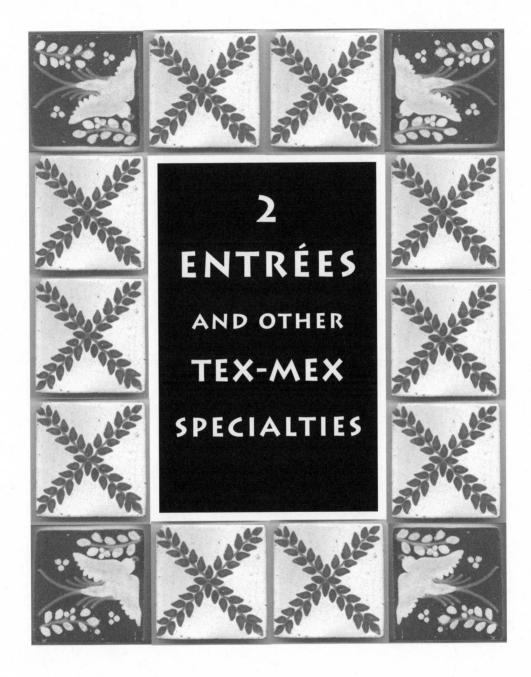

2
ENTRÉES
AND OTHER
TEX-MEX
SPECIALTIES

ENTRÉES AND OTHER TEX-MEX SPECIALTIES:
FAJITAS TO BARBACOA

SOUP

Going back to both its Indian and Spanish roots, Mexico has a strong tradition of soups, many of which are of the meal-in-itself variety. Virtually all are made entirely of fresh ingredients. Tex-Mex cooks maintained the tradition, but adapted it to ingredients available within their means.

The result is that many Tex-Mex soups are basically brothy stews of beef or chicken. Many are good, but rarely great. However, the following version of tortilla soup and *caldo xochhitl* are a cut above, and make great soup courses or light suppers.

TORTILLA SOUP

Tortilla soup now means just about any soupy concoction that contains crisp-fried corn tortilla strips. This version is not just one of the best and easiest, but is also infinitely adaptable for use with other ingredients. For example, try substituting the tortilla chips with 2 cups of canned *pozole* (hominy) and the cheese with three-quarters of a pound of cubed, medium-firm tofu. The result is both healthy and delicious.

The sweet flavor of caramelized onions is important to the dish, but if you are in a hurry simply cook them just until they are soft. Getting the chile strips cooked to the proper degree is also important. They should be very dark and crisp, but not scorched.

Tortilla Soup

Oil for deep frying
4 corn tortillas cut into strips about 2 inches long and
     between 1/8- and 1/4-inch wide
1 cup grated mozzarella cheese
2 tablespoons olive oil
2 *ancho* chiles, stemmed, seeded and cut into 1/8-inch strips
1 whole, medium white onion, sliced thinly (about 2 1/2
     cups)
2 cloves minced garlic
1 14 1/2-ounce can whole tomatoes, unsalted if possible
4 cups chicken broth
Water
1 cup chopped zucchini
1 cup chopped crookneck squash
1 teaspoon dried thyme
1/2 teaspoon black pepper
3/4 teaspoon salt, or to taste
1 tablespoon lime juice
3 tablespoons chopped cilantro
1 avocado, peeled, pitted, and sliced
1/4 cup sour cream

Heat the oil to between 345 and 350 degrees and fry the tortilla strips in batches until they are a crisp golden brown. Drain them on absorbent towels and place equal portions in each of 4 large soup bowls. Put equal portions of the cheese on top of the tortilla strips. In a large pot, heat the olive oil over medium heat. Add the *ancho* chile strips and fry them until they just begin to turn dark and become crisp, 30 seconds to 1 minute, then put them into the bowls on top of the tortilla chips and cheese. Do not allow them to overcook, as they will quickly become bitter.

Add the onion slices to the oil and fry them, stirring frequently, until they are golden brown, reducing the heat and adding additional oil as necessary, about 15 to 20 minutes. Turn the heat to low and add the garlic. Cook, stirring constantly, for a minute or two, or until the garlic is soft.

While the onions are cooking, blend the canned tomatoes, including their juice, to a puree, and then pour them into a 2-quart measuring cup. Add the chicken broth and enough water to equal a total of 6 cups.

When the onions are done, pour the tomato mixture into the pot, add both squashes, the thyme and the pepper and bring to a boil. Simmer the soup for 5 minutes, add the salt, lime juice and cilantro. Simmer another minute, then serve over the cheese, tortilla and chile strips. Top with the avocado and a dollop of sour cream.

Serves 4.

CALDO XOCHITL
(Fresh Chicken-and-Vegetable Soup)

*C*aldo xochitl (pronounced: call-doh show-sheet-til) is a soup from Mexico's interior whose ingredients are just cooked through. Unlike the usual Tex-Mex versions of Mexican soups, it has a light freshness, with vegetables that are not stewed into oblivion. It is intended to serve as a luncheon or light supper dish, so the ratio of solid ingredients to liquid is fairly high. It can be converted to a more elegant first course by reducing the vegetables or adding additional broth.

This soup will be only as good as its broth, which means using a homemade one. The liquid used to make the shredded chicken filling, which is also part of the recipe, is a good choice. If you do use a canned broth be sure to reduce the salt as necessary. So that all the ingredients are cooked to the proper degree, it is also important to cut the vegetables into the specified sizes.

Caldo Xochitl

8 ounces shredded chicken (see recipe index) about 1 1/2 cups
1 1/2 cups steamed white rice, or Mexican-style rice (see recipe index)
1 cup yellow summer squash, cut into 1/4-inch dice
1 cup zucchini, cut into 1/4-inch dice
1 Roma tomato cut into 1/4-inch dice
1/2 cup carrot cut into 1/8-inch dice
2 green onions, very finely chopped
1/4 cup peeled jicama cut into 1/8-inch dice
2 *serrano* chiles, minced, or substitute jalapeños
3 cups chicken broth
3/4 to 1 teaspoon salt, or to taste
1 avocado, cut into 3/4 inch pieces
1/4 cup loosely packed, chopped cilantro
2/3 cup grated cotija cheese, or substitute Parmesan
Lime wedges

Mix the chicken, rice, squash, zucchini, tomato, carrot, green onions, jicama and chiles in a bowl. Bring the broth to a boil in a large pot over high heat, add the chicken, rice, and mixed vegetables, return to a boil and simmer until the carrots are just tender but still have texture, about 1 minute. Quickly add salt to taste, and ladle the soup into bowls.

Put equal portions of the avocado into each bowl, sprinkle the cilantro and cheese over the soup and serve with the lime wedges.

Serves 4 as a light meal.

EGGS

For the most part, with the exception of breakfast tacos and *huevos rancheros,* egg dishes are more popular in Tex-Mex home-style cooking than in restaurants. In homes, eggs are fried, poached and scrambled and served with different chile sauces, bacon, chorizo and other meats and cheeses. But for our purposes, a really good version of *huevos rancheros* defines the genre, and that is what you will find below.

HUEVOS RANCHEROS
(Ranch-Style Eggs)

In addition to being the most popular egg dish in Mexican cooking, *huevos rancheros* is also one that's jumped the fence to the point that it can often be found not just in Mexican restaurants but also in coffee shops and breakfast specialty chains throughout the United States.

Huevos rancheros consists of fried eggs placed on a lightly-fried corn tortilla and topped with a tomato and chile *salsa ranchera,* from which it derives its name. In Mexico, *ranchero* sauces are often made with fresh tomatoes, but in Tex-Mex cooking they are more often made from canned tomatoes.

This is a good time to set aside the political correctness that leads us to reject anything not made from fresh—not to mention organic—ingredients.

Just as some of the best Italian cooked tomato sauces are at least partially made with canned tomatoes, so are some of those from Mexico. The truth is that canned tomatoes produce cooked sauces that are often sweeter and thicker than those made from fresh tomatoes. And the unpleasant canned flavor disappears to a large extent during the cooking process. This does not mean that fresh tomatoes are not often the best choice, such as in the sauce for *chiles rellenos,* just that canned tomatoes should not be automatically rejected.

One caveat: I suggest you use whole canned tomatoes (unsalted, if possible) and do not even think about using stewed tomatoes.

Since you want your fried eggs to sit neatly on a corn tortilla, I suggest you use an egg ring. While it is not necessary, it does make the job easier and yields a nice presentation. An egg ring is a 5-inch circle of steel with a handle that is placed in a skillet and into which two large eggs are broken. It causes the two eggs to cook in a perfect circle slightly smaller than most corn tortillas. To use it, first break two eggs carefully into a small dish. Then melt a little butter in a skillet, place the ring in the skillet and pour the eggs into its center. If you cannot find this handy device in regular stores, check with the nearest restaurant supplier. It also helps to use a Teflon-coated skillet.

Huevos rancheros are traditionally served with refried beans, but they are delicious with hashbrowns as well. A special touch is to top the sauce with a dollop of *crema mexicana,* which is very similar to *crème fraîche.* An excellent substitute is made by mixing a little whipping cream with sour cream.

Huevos Rancheros

The sauce:
2 14 1/2-ounce cans whole tomatoes (unsalted, if possible)
2 tablespoons olive oil
1 cup chopped white onion
3 jalapeño peppers, stemmed, seeded and chopped
2 cloves minced garlic
3 tablespoons tomato paste

1 teaspoon dried oregano
1/3 cup loosely packed, chopped cilantro
2 tablespoons chopped fresh parsley
1/4 teaspoon ground black pepper
Salt, to taste (approximately 1/2 teaspoon if using unsalted
    tomatoes)

Remove the tomatoes from the cans, reserving the juice, and chop them coarsely, either by hand or, more conveniently, in a food processor. Heat the oil in a medium saucepan over medium heat, add the onion and jalapeños and cook, stirring frequently, until they are soft but not yet beginning to brown.

Add the garlic and continue cooking, stirring constantly, for 1 minute. Before the garlic can scorch, add the chopped tomatoes, then stir in the reserved juice from the cans, the tomato paste, oregano, cilantro, parsley and pepper.

Adjust the heat to a low simmer and continue cooking, stirring frequently, until the sauce has thickened (about 15 minutes), then add salt to taste. The sauce can be prepared several days ahead and kept refrigerated.

The eggs:
Ranchero sauce
8 large eggs
cooking oil
4 corn tortillas
Butter
1/2 cup *crème fraîche,* or substitute 5 tablespoons sour cream
    mixed with 3 tablespoons whipping cream

Heat the ranchero sauce and keep it warm while you prepare the eggs. Break two eggs into each of 4 small dishes (teacups work well) and reserve.

To prepare the tortillas, heat about 1/4 inch of oil in the bottom of a skillet just slightly larger than the tortillas over medium heat. When a drop of water sputters instantly in the oil, cook the tortillas, one at a time, on each side until just firm but not crisp. Drain the tortillas and place one on each of 4 serving plates.

Heat a skillet over medium heat, melt a little butter, and cook the eggs 2 at time, either sunny-side-up or over, as you like them. Place each pair of cooked eggs on a tortilla, and cover with the sauce and a tablespoon or two of the cream mixture. Serve with refried beans (see recipe index).

Serves 4.

FAJITAS

South Texas restaurateurs made fajitas a national food craze by literally selling the sizzle. And what used to mean the particular cut of beef called skirt steak can now refer to nearly anything. So-called chicken fajitas are as common as expensive coffee places, and sirloin, shrimp, fish, lamb, pork and even asparagus and eggplant fajitas turn up as well. Restaurants have learned that their customers will eagerly eat almost anything as long as it is charbroiled, cut into little pieces and served on a smoking-hot platter.

To be precise, the name fajitas should be applied only to skirt steak; everything else should be referred to in terms such as "chicken, fajita style."

Like so many other aspects of Mexican cooking, there are unexpected subtleties in the seemingly simple preparation of fajitas. For example, most of the skirt steak available in supermarkets is tough. (That's why it was made into hamburger until South Texans sold the sizzle.) To prepare skirt steak for fajitas requires considerable tenderizing. This can be accomplished by machine (which ruins the texture), through a marinade (which affects the taste) or with a powdered tenderizer. If you decide to use the latter, I strongly recommend Adolph's® All Natural, No MSG, Sodium Free, Original Unseasoned. It does a good job without materially affecting the flavor.

There is, however, another solution that has been a carefully guarded secret. Most supermarket skirt steak comes from the inside cut. That, of course, infers that there is an outside cut. There is, and it is night and day more tender than the inside cut, which consists of fairly wide pieces found on the inside near the cow's stomach; the outside pieces are more narrow and found, as one would imagine, outside, close to the skin.

But can you get it? The outside cut skirt steak is available in some South Texas markets, but it can be difficult to find elsewhere. Just ask your butcher, bearing in mind that he or she may not even know that there are two different cuts.

If you cannot find the outside cut, there is yet another option, though one that some purists consider cheating. There is a sirloin flap cut that looks exactly like a skirt steak. It is much more tender than the inside cut skirt steak, with much the same flavor and texture as the outside cut. Unfortunately, it too may be difficult to find.

To be authentic, fajitas should be natural, both in flavor and in texture, with nothing added but some salt and pepper, a touch of lime juice and the kiss of mesquite smoke. If you cannot find the outside cut of the skirt steak or the sirloin substitute, I suggest you use the powdered tenderizer, which will make the meat much more tender without materially affecting the taste.

Although fajitas can be cooked over charcoal or any hardwood, on a gas grill, or pan-broiled in a ridged-iron or regular skillet, the authentic treatment requires either mesquite charcoal or wood. The only alternative I do not recommend is to pan-broil them on a flat surface. While, even in Texas, this method is used, especially for a crowd, it produces a less tender, less flavorful and altogether less interesting result.

To get the proper char, fajitas should be cooked over a very hot fire. This can be achieved by using mesquite charcoal set 4 to 5 inches from the grill or with regular charcoal about 2 to 3 inches from the grill. If you have a grill with a cover it is best not to close it as it will lower the temperature.

Because the skirt steak is quite dense it takes somewhat longer to cook than a regular cut, such as a top sirloin. For example, a skirt steak that is about one-half inch thick takes about the same time to reach the desired degree of doneness as a 3/4- to 1-inch sirloin. This is an advantage, as it allows the thinner fajita to char a bit on the outside before it is overdone.

Fajitas are usually broiled whole then sliced into small pieces, against the grain for maximum tenderness. With a skirt steak, which is long and thin, the grain goes sideways across the short side. This means that you will need to cut the cooked steak into pieces about 2 to 3 inches in length, then slice them into pieces about 1/4 to 1/2 an inch wide against the grain, which is along what was initially the long side.

Fajitas are traditionally served sizzling on a hot iron platter topped with caramelized onions. You can achieve the same effect by placing the cut meat in a very hot iron skillet, topping it with the cooked onions and sprinkling on some lime juice, which creates the steam and sizzle.

Fajitas

2 pounds skirt steak, outside cut, if possible
Adolph's® All Natural, No MSG, Sodium Free, Original
      Unseasoned tenderizer (optional with the outside cut)
Salt and black pepper to taste
3 tablespoons lime juice
1 dozen flour tortillas
Guacamole
Pico de gallo
Salsa

If using tenderizer, apply it just before you start the coals. To do this, sprinkle it over one side and drive it into the meat by puncturing it all over with a fork. This mimics the action of a machine tenderizer, but, as it is not nearly as aggressive, does not ruin the texture. Turn the meat over and repeat on the other side. Salt and pepper the meat to taste.

Start a fire as close to the grill as possible, using either mesquite charcoal or wood. The coals will be ready within a few minutes after the flames subside. Before placing the meat on the grill, allow it to become very hot and brush it quickly with the end of a towel dipped in cooking oil to keep the meat from sticking.

If you want to serve the fajitas with the onions, prepare them just after you light the coals (see below).

To broil the meat, place it over the coals and allow it to cook for about 2 minutes, then turn and repeat on the other side. Depending on the heat of your coals and the distance from the grill, you may need to turn the meat again and cook another minute or two. If you plan to serve the fajitas in a sizzling hot skillet, make them a little less well-done than you want them, as they will continue to cook in the pan.

When the fajitas are finished, remove them from the heat, place them on a chopping board, and allow them to rest for 2-3 minutes. This will allow them to reabsorb their juices, so that they will not all run out when the meat is cut.

In the meantime, heat an iron skillet over high heat until it is very hot, but do not get it so hot that it might break. Also, place the tortillas, guacamole, pico de gallo and salsa on the table. Slice the meat against the grain as described above, mix it with the reserved onions, if using them, and scrape the combination into the skillet. Immediately pour the lime juice over the meat.

Serve the platter of sizzling fajitas, making sure you use kitchen mitts or thick layers of towel to protect your hands from the heat and something like a small chopping block under the pan to protect your table surface.

Serves 4.

The optional onions:
2 tablespoons olive oil
1 large white onion, cut into thin slices
1 clove minced garlic
1/2 teaspoon dried thyme
2 tablespoons finely chopped cilantro

Heat a large skillet over medium heat, add the olive oil, then the onions and toss them thoroughly. Cook the onions, stirring frequently, until they are golden brown. To keep them from burning turn the heat down as necessary. This should take about 20 minutes. Just before the onions are done, add the garlic, thyme and cilantro and cook two minutes more. Scrape the onions into a bowl and reserve.

CHICKEN FAJITA-STYLE

Calling this dish chicken fajitas, as is usually the case, is akin to calling it something like chicken sirloin. The reason is that fajitas refers specifically to the cut of beef called skirt steak. However, the chicken version, whatever it is called, is a terrific alternative or complement to real fajitas.

Made by char-broiling boneless, skinless chicken breasts, then slicing and serving them on a sizzling platter, they evoke much the same effect as the original, but with a lot less fat. The two also go well together, giving diners a real choice with very little extra trouble.

Since boneless, skinless chicken breast can be a little dry and tough if even slightly overcooked, this dish benefits from a marinade such as the one below. As with beef fajitas, chicken fajita-style is frequently served with caramelized onions.

Chicken fajita style

The marinade:
1/3 cup lime juice
3 cloves garlic, coarsely chopped
2 teaspoons salt
1/2 tablespoon chile powder
1/4 teaspoon black pepper
2 teaspoons dried oregano
1 jalapeño, stemmed, seeded and coarsely chopped
1 cup cooking oil

The chicken:
2 pounds boneless, skinless, chicken breasts
3 tablespoons lime juice
1 dozen flour tortillas
Guacamole
Pico de gallo
Salsa

Place the 1/3 cup lime juice, garlic, salt, chile powder, black pepper, oregano and jalapeño in a blender and blend until completely pureed, about 1 minute. Add the oil and blend briefly to thoroughly combine. Pour the marinade over the chicken breasts and marinate, refrigerated, for 1 hour, but no more than 1 1/2 hours or the lime juice will begin to chemically cook the chicken, as with ceviche.

Light your coals or fire up a gas grill so it they will be ready when the chicken has been marinated, allowing about 25 minutes for coals and 15 minutes for gas.

If you want to serve the fajitas with the onions, begin to prepare them just after you light the coals.

Drain the marinade from the chicken and grill it until it is golden brown on both sides and just cooked through. This is very important, as overcooking will cause the chicken to be dry and tough. With practice you can tell by the feel, but until then cut into it with a paring knife and remove it from the grill as soon as the last trace of pink disappears.

If you are going to serve the chicken in a hot skillet, remove it just before all the pink is gone, as it will continue to cook on the hot surface. Slice the chicken breasts sideways into 1/4-inch pieces.

To serve, heat an iron skillet over medium high heat until very hot, mix the chicken with the reserved onions if using them, and place the combination into the skillet. Immediately pour the 3 tablespoons of lime juice over the meat. Serve the platter, making sure you use a hot glove or thick layers of towel to protect your hands from the heat, and something like a small chopping block under the pan to protect your table. Serve with the tortillas, guacamole, pico de gallo and salsa.

Serves 4.

The optional onions:
2 tablespoons olive oil
1 large white onion, cut into thin slices
1 clove minced garlic
1/2 teaspoon dried thyme
2 tablespoons finely chopped cilantro

Heat a large skillet over medium heat, add the olive oil, then the onions, and toss them thoroughly. Cook the onions, stirring frequently until they are golden brown. To keep them from burning turn the heat down as necessary. This should take about 20 minutes. Just before the onions are done, add the garlic, thyme and cilantro and cook two minutes more. Scrape the onions into a bowl and reserve.

AGUJAS
(Eye of Chuck Steaks)

The word *agujas* translates to "needles" in English, and probably refers to the long thin bone of this cut of meat. Taken from the eye of chuck, this unpretentious but delicious steak was first popularized in northern Mexico, where restaurants often sell it at the same price as filet mignon. The almost forgotten, beefy taste of the chuck more than makes up for the fact that it is tougher than the more usual cuts such as New Yorks and ribeyes. It is a terrific version of *carne asada*. Unless you live in an area where this cut is sold by name, simply ask a butcher to cut steaks about an inch thick from the eye of chuck.

Agujas are almost always seasoned with salt and pepper and char-broiled over mesquite wood or charcoal, but that is where the consensus ends. Some cooks broil it for a short time over very hot coals, and others cook it for much longer over low coals. I use a third method, more closely aligned with the first, and one that produces a crispy exterior and a moist, tender interior. That method involves cooking the meat directly on mesquite coals without using a grill. While logic dictates that putting meat directly on red-hot coals will cause it to be irretrievably charred, that does not happen, and cooking it is actually a lot of fun.

With this approach, always use either mesquite or another charcoal made from hardwood. Briquettes are often made with petroleum products, and meat that comes in direct conact with them when being cooked is just not appealing. This cut does well with a little un-flavored meat tenderizer.

Agujas

4 1/2-inch steaks cut from the eye of chuck
2 tablespoons fresh lime juice
Powdered meat tenderizer made without salt or MSG
    (Adolph's® All Natural, No MSG, Sodium Free, Original
    Unseasoned is a good choice)
Kosher salt and freshly ground black pepper, to taste
Mesquite charcoal or charcoal from another hardwood

Brush a little lime juice on both sides of the steaks. Coat both sides with a sprinkling of tenderizer, then pierce them all over (avoiding the bones) with a fork. Sprinkle on some salt and pepper on one side, and set them aside while you prepare the fire.

Light enough of the charcoal so that after it burns to coals a reasonably flat surface can be formed that will accommodate all the steaks at one time. After the charcoal has burned down to glowing coals, using long cooking tongs or other barbecue tools push them into that relatively flat surface.

To broil the steaks, place them, seasoned side down, directly on the coals for 2 1/2 to 3 minutes, or until they are a crispy, golden brown. Turn the steaks and broil until they are a bit crusty on the other sides and done as you like them, about 2 to 3 minutes. Serve the *agujas* with Mexican rice and/or refried beans or *frijoles a la charra,* guacamole, flour tortillas and *pico de gallo.*

Serves 4.

BIFTEC RANCHERO
(Ranch-Style Steak)

Really another version of *carne asada,* this dish uses the popular *salsa ranchero* or ranch-style sauce over steaks, and has so many options that you can basically make the recipe your own. You can use nearly any popular cut of steak—ribeye, New York, sirloin, tenderloin, skirt, etc. The steaks can be as thick or thin as you like, they can be grilled over coals or pan-broiled and you can top them with cheese, either before or just after you top them with the hot sauce.

My advice is that, if the steaks are less than 3/4 of an inch thick it makes sense to pan-broil them, particularly if you want them to be medium rare to rare and still be crusty on the outside. This is perhaps the more common approach, and the one used in the following recipe.

If the steaks are thicker than 3/4 inch, you can grill them until browned on the outside and still not overdone in the center.

Biftek ranchero makes an easy, quick meal that is especially delicious served with refried beans and rice.

Biftek Ranchero

1 1/2 to 2 tablespoons vegetable oil
4 ribeye or other steaks cut to 1/2-inch thick
1 recipe ranchero sauce (see recipe index)
2 cups shredded mozzarella or Monterey Jack cheese

Bring the ranchero sauce to a boil, then keep it just below a simmer while you prepare the steaks. Heat a griddle or heavy skillet over medium-high to high heat, add enough of the vegetable oil to thoroughly coat the bottom, add the steaks and cook, turning once or twice, until they are well browned on the outside and done as you like them in the middle.

Place the steaks on serving plates, top with half the cheese, top with the ranchero sauce, then with the remaining cheese. Serve the steaks with refried beans and/or Mexican rice.

Serves 4.

Chuletas de Puerco Ranchero (Pork Chops Ranchero)

To prepare this dish simply follow the directions for *Biftec Ranchero*, substituting either center-cut or rib-cut pork chops for the steak. As with the steak recipe, thinner cuts of pork lend themselves to pan-broiling while the thicker variety can be either pan or char broiled.

STEAK AND ENCHILADAS

Although I had rarely found this dish in restaurants before moving to San Antonio, I served it frequently at home. Upon arriving in San Antonio, I discovered it to be a popular restaurant dish. It is now one of my favorite Tex-Mex entrees.

Although it can be made with thin slices of tenderloin, New York, fajitas or even T-bone, my favorite is a boneless ribeye. This cut has enough fat so that the very thin meat remains juicy even if well-done. Whatever cut you use, serve them with your favorite enchiladas—cheese-filled ones with either red or green chile sauce are favorites.

Just sear the steaks on either a ridged grill pan or skillet and place them next to the enchiladas (1 or 2 per person). Add some Mexican rice, refried beans and lettuce garnish and you have a special combination that makes a terrific entree.

Steak and Enchiladas

4 thin-cut steaks (1/2 inch or less)
Cooking oil
4 to 8 enchiladas of any variety (see recipe index)
Mexican rice (optional)
Refried beans (optional)
Lettuce and tomato garnish

Just before the enchiladas come out of the oven, sear the steaks to brown on one side over high heat on a grill pan or skillet. If you use a skillet, first add just enough cooking oil to coat the pan.

If you will be serving the enchiladas on oven-hot plates, turn the steaks and barely sear them on the other side, as they will continue to cook on the hot surfaces. Otherwise, continue cooking the steaks until they are done as you wish. Place the steaks on the plates next to the enchiladas, add the remaining items, if you wish, and serve.

Serves 4.

CARNE GUISADA

This is the classic Tex-Mex chile stew. Although made with many of the same ingredients, it differs considerably from Texas-style chile in that it is much milder with more subtle flavors. It can be served as a stew or used as a filling for tacos or burritos. It is particularly delicious served wrapped in hot flour tortillas.

Carne Guisada

2 tablespoons olive oil
2 pounds very lean stew meat cut into 3/4-inch chunks
1 cup white onion, chopped
1 jalapeño pepper, stemmed, seeded and coarsely chopped
2 cloves garlic, minced
1 cup chopped tomato
1 tablespoon chile powder
1/2 teaspoon ground cumin
1/4 cup tomato sauce
Salt and pepper to taste
1 tablespoon plus 1 teaspoon cooking oil
2 tablespoons flour

Brown the meat in the cooking oil over medium high heat. You will probably have to do this in two batches so as not to over-crowd the pan, which impedes browning.

Remove the meat, and turn the burner to medium. Add the onion, jalapeño and garlic and cook until the vegetables begin to soften. Return the meat to the pot, add the tomato, chile powder and cumin and cook for 30 seconds. Stir in the tomato sauce and enough water to cover the contents of the pot and simmer, covered, for about 1 hour and 45 minutes, or until the meat is very tender.

When the dish is completed there should be just enough liquid remaining to come about half way up the meat, so check occasionally and add more water if necessary.

Just before the stew is done, make the roux. Heat the oil over medium heat, add the flour and, whisking it constantly, cook until it begins to turn golden. Then remove it from the heat and reserve. When the stew is done, whisk 1 teaspoon of the roux into the liquid at a time, continuing to simmer for about 30 seconds. Continue adding more roux until the liquid is thick enough to make a gravy that coats the back of a spoon.

Serves 4.

SOUTH-TEXAS-STYLE BEEF BARBACOA

The ancient tradition of *barbacoa* runs deep within Mexico. It is also alive and well in South Texas, where the large Mexican-American population has made significant contributions to the culture of the entire area.

However, even in places like San Antonio, where one cannot drive far without passing a restaurant specializing in this dish, barbacoa is not universally understood. There is the vague notion that it is some sort of mysterious Mexican barbecue made with equally ambiguous ingredients. Even recent arrivals from Mexico can be perplexed because the Tex-Mex barbacoa differs from that traditionally found in Mexico.

In South Texas, *barbacoa* is most often made with parts from the head of a cow, such as the cheeks, some of which will no longer be permitted on the market based on regulations prompted by the risk of mad cow disease. But never fear, our recipe will capture the essence of the original with a normal, permissible cut; no mystery meat in this recipe!

In northern Mexico, *barbacoa* is also sometimes made with the head of a cow, but more often it is prepared with *cabrito* (kid). In central Mexico, the meat of choice is lamb, and in the Yucatan their traditional version, *cochinita pibil* (pit-style pork) is prepared with pork.

Perhaps even greater than the difference between the main ingredient in the Tex-Mex version of *barbacoa* and those in Mexico's interior is the cooking process. Throughout Mexico, traditional *barbacoa* is usually made in the same way it was for centuries before the arrival of the Spanish. In this original, Indian pit-cooking process, the meat is seasoned, wrapped in either maguey (agave) or banana leaves, then placed on a grill over a cauldron of water set over glowing coals in a pit about three feet deep. Often beans, other vegetables, and spices are added to the pot, and will later be served as a soup with the meat. The pit is then covered and sealed with damp earth.

The result is that the meat cooks in a unique process combining both smoke and steam. Through the magic of culinary alchemy it emerges falling-apart tender, and infused with smoky flavor.

In and around San Antonio, *barbacoa* is often made with only half the process. Usually, meat from the cow's head is steamed in special steel vessels rather than smoked over water in the traditional manner, although it should be noted that some commercial producers in Mexico also have forsaken the traditional pit.

Why San Antonio's *barbacoa* is so often steamed without the flavorful addition of smoke is an open question. In response to the query, more than one *barbacoa* restaurant proprietor replied that the Health Department would not permit the traditional method. However, when pressed, they were unable to supply specific reasons.

A subsequent conversation with one of the city's health inspectors elicited the opinion that there is no reason why a method that mimics the traditional process could not be used. Certainly pits of bare earth would not be permitted, but other more hygiene-friendly methods could be used. The inspector surmised that steaming might be popular because it is less expensive and less time consuming.

Fortunately, for those who may not live near a *barbacoa* outlet, or who want that extra kiss of smoke, there is a safe and easy method of producing Tex-Mex (or any other style) *barbacoa* at home with familiar supermarket cuts. A significant advantage of the technique, which uses a relatively inexpensive water smoker, is that it can be used to make other types of regional barbeque, including Texas-style beef brisket, ribs and Carolina pulled-pork, and do so much more easily than with traditional methods. A water smoker can also be used to reheat tamales for 15 to 20 minutes, giving them a crispy texture, and delicious, smoky flavor.

Water smokers can be purchased at many hardware, building product and barbecue stores for between $50 and $180. They come in different models that rely alternately on charcoal, electricity and propane gas to provide the heat. Electric models are the easiest to use since charcoal models require careful measuring of the fuel and addition of coals during cooking to maintain the proper temperature. Gas smokers require the use of propane, which can run out during cooking. Electric models need only be plugged into an outdoor electrical outlet.

The cooking process for an electric water smoker is one I found in an article in *Cook's Illustrated* magazine on Southern pulled-pork barbecue. It goes as follows: A few chunks or a handful of chips of soaked hardwood, such as mesquite or hickory, is placed in the bottom of the smoker on or near the heating element, according to the manufacturer's instructions. The water dish is filled with water, the meat is placed on the grill, the top put on the smoker and its cord plugged into an ordinary household outlet.

About 4 hours later the meat is removed, sealed in a foil baking dish, and placed in a medium oven for 1 hour and 45 minutes. The foil package is then removed from the oven and enclosed in a paper grocery bag for an additional 45 minutes.

The result is a magical transformation that produces meat that literally falls off the bone, and mimics traditional *barbacoa* in that it combines smoke and steam heat. While the cooking time is about six hours, active preparation requires only about 30 minutes.

The following recipe for South-Texas-style *barbacoa* uses the popular, readily available chuck roast.

South Texas Style Beef Barbacoa

1 1/2 teaspoons garlic powder
1 1/2 teaspoons black pepper
1 tablespoon dried oregano
1 1/2 teaspoons chile powder
1 teaspoon salt, or to taste
A 2 1/2 to 3 1/2 pound bone-in chuck roast

Just before cooking, mix together the first five ingredients and rub them all over the meat.

Place some soaked wood chips near the heating element of a water smoker, according to the manufacturer's instructions. Pour 3 quarts boiling water into the water pan, and smoke the pork for 4 hours at between 225 and 275 degrees. Check the smoker after 2 hours and add additional boiling water to the pan, if necessary.

When done, the internal temperature of the beef should be 160 to 170 degrees. Place the beef in a baking pan (a disposable foil pan works well), seal it with heavy-duty aluminum foil and place it in an oven preheated to 325 degrees. Bake for 1 hour and 45 minutes.

Remove the package from the oven and place it in a large, paper, grocery bag, fold the bag tightly to seal it and let it rest for 45 minutes. If your foil pan is too large for one bag, use two, over-lapping them to completely cover the pan.

Remove the meat from the roasting pan. It will literally fall off the bone! Chop and shred the meat into small pieces. Serve with guacamole, salsa, and hot tortillas.

Serves 4 to 6.

COUNTRY-STYLE SPARE RIBS

In classic Tex-Mex fashion, this recipe takes an inexpensive ingredient and transforms it into something delicious with many uses.

Now that pork is being produced so lean that it is barely recognizable as the pork of 20 years ago, boneless country-style ribs—while a little fatty—do a good job of recreating a nearly forgotten taste and tenderness. These ribs can be served as an entree, they can be cut into bite-size pieces and served as a stew, or they can be shredded and used as a filling for anything from tacos to enchiladas.

Country-Style Spare Ribs

The sauce:
2 *ancho* chiles, stemmed and seeded
4 cloves garlic
1/2 teaspoon dried oregano
1 teaspoon dried thyme
2 cups water
3/4 cup orange juice
1/2 teaspoon salt

Soak the chiles in hot water to cover for 20 minutes, drain and place them in a blender. Add the garlic, oregano, thyme and water and blend for 2 minutes. Add the orange juice and salt, blend briefly to combine, then reserve.

The ribs:

2 pounds boneless, country-style pork ribs

Salt and pepper to taste

1 1/2 tablespoons cooking oil

The reserved sauce

Preheat your oven to 325 degrees.

Salt and pepper the ribs on both sides. Heat the oil in a skillet, baking dish or Dutch oven (one that can be placed in the oven) over medium-high to high heat. Cook the seasoned ribs on all sides until they are a crusty golden-brown. Remove the hot dish from the heat and allow it to cool for a few seconds, then pour off the fat in the pan and discard. (If you do not do this the dish will be overly fatty). Pour just enough of the sauce into the dish to barely cover the meat, then replace the pan on the heat.

Bring the liquid to a low simmer, then place the uncovered pan in the oven. Bake, spooning a little of the sauce over the top of the meat about every 15 minutes, for 1 1/4 to 1 1/2 hours.

Using oven mitts, remove the pan. If the sauce is still runny, place it on the stove over medium heat and simmer it until it is fairly thick. Add salt to taste.

The ribs can be served whole with some sauce on top, cut into 1-inch pieces and mixed with the sauce as a stew, or shredded with a little of the sauce to make a delicious filling for tacos and other items.

Serves 4.

MILANESA

In Mexico, *milanesa* is a dish adapted from the famous Italian veal specialty that is coated with bread crumbs and fried to a crisp golden-brown. It is made with veal and pork, or with thinly sliced beef in northern Mexico.

In Tex-Mex cooking, *milanesa* is usually made with beef—a Mexican version of chicken fried steak—although I prefer it made with pork, which is more tender and just as flavorful. *Milanesa* is delicious topped with *ranchero* sauce and served with Mexican-style rice.

Because of the lack of uniformity in the cuts of meat, the pieces you use will be of different sizes. After they have been pounded very thin, simply use whatever pieces you think will fit well on your serving plates.

Around Saltillo, in northern Mexico, *milanesa* is often used as a filling for tacos, made using the semi-crisp corn tortillas described in the recipe for Tex-Mex tacos and topping the meat with guacamole and salsa.

Milanesa

1 pound round steak, sliced 1/8 inch thick or less, or substitute pork loin or leg
2 cups milk
1 1/2 teaspoons chile powder
1 teaspoon salt
2 cups flour
1 1/2 teaspoons salt
4 1/2 teaspoons chile powder
2 teaspoons garlic powder
Cooking oil
Ranchero sauce (optional) (see recipe index)

Place the pieces of meat between sheets of plastic wrap on a chopping block. Carefully pound them with a meat pounder or the back of a small iron skillet until they are well under 1/8-inch thick.

Place the meat in a bowl. Mix together the milk, 1 1/2 teaspoons chile powder and salt, pour it over the meat and refrigerate for 1 hour. Mix together the flour, salt, 4 1/2 teaspoons chile powder and garlic powder in a shallow dish. Drain each piece of meat and dredge it in the flour mixture. Refrigerate for 15 minutes, then again dip the meat in the milk mixture, coat with flour, and refrigerate for another 15 minutes.

To cook the meat, pour about 3/4 of an inch of the oil in a large skillet and heat over medium to medium-high heat until it is very hot, but not smoking. Fry the meat, turning once, until it is golden-brown and cooked through. If you wish, top the milanesa with heated *ranchero* sauce and serve with steamed squash and Mexican rice.

Serves 4.

CARNITAS

Carnitas is one of those dishes that is nearly always found wherever Mexican food is popular. Although the word literally means "little meats," *carnitas* almost always refers to chunks of pork that are simmered in large quantities of lard. The result is crunchy, tender, flavorful golden-brown pieces of meat, similar to a French *confit. Carnitas* are traditionally eaten as an entree with corn tortillas, guacamole and salsa, but also make a terrific filling for tacos and burritos.

Many restaurants actually bake or braise their *carnitas,* and the results, while different from the those obtained with the traditional method, are no less delicious.

The following recipe uses milk rather than lard to simmer the pork and produces a terrific result. However, if you wish to use the traditional method, simply cook the pork at a bare simmer in melted lard to cover for about 1 1/4 hours, or until it is very tender and golden brown.

Please note that our pork has become so lean that carnitas, while they can be made from a loin cut, are at their best when made with the fattier pork butt. The cut I favor is boneless country-style pork ribs.

Carnitas

2 1/2 tablespoons olive oil
2 pounds boneless country-style pork ribs, or meat from
      another part of the pork butt, cut into 3/4-inch chunks
1 1/4 cups milk
1 teaspoon dried thyme
3 cloves garlic, finely chopped
Salt to taste

Heat the olive oil in a large pot over medium heat, add the pork and cook, stirring every 30 seconds until the meat is browned all over, about 5 minutes. Add the milk, thyme and garlic and bring the milk to a bare simmer.

Continue simmering the meat, stirring about every 5 minutes, until all the liquid has evaporated, adjusting the heat as necessary to keep the simmer very low, about 1 3/4 hours. The milk will appear curdled but don't worry.

When all the liquid is gone and the meat begins to sizzle in the rendered fat, turn the heat slightly higher and continue cooking, stirring often, until each piece of meat is golden brown, about 10 minutes, but do not allow it to scorch. Sprinkle on salt to taste and serve the *carnitas* with corn tortillas, guacamole and salsa, or coarsely chop and use it as a filling for tacos.

Serves 4.

QUAIL or DOVE,
FRIED or BOILED

Dove hunting is a South Texas tradition, and hunting quail is also popular. From Texans with their own ranches to those who simply have a friend with some acreage outside the city limits, men and, yes, women, gather in September for the yearly ritual.

In years gone by wild game was a necessary source of sustenance on ranches, but now the tradition is carried on more for sport. Although not found in restaurants in Texas as often as they are in northern Mexico, these game birds are nevertheless an important part of the Tex-Mex tradition.

While doves are not usually available in grocery stores, farm-raised quails are often available. These birds can be broiled or fried, but are so small that broiling can often lead to a dry, tough result. To minimize this, I recommend first marinating them, then wrapping them in bacon. For frying, the traditional method is the same as for milanesa.

Broiled Doves or Quail

8 cleaned and plucked doves or quail
1/4 cup lime juice
1 tablespoon chile powder
1 teaspoon Worcestershire sauce
1 teaspoon salt
1 1/2 cups cooking oil
8 pieces bacon
Toothpicks

Place the birds on a chopping block and flatten them with the palm of your hand or the back of a small iron skillet. Mix together the lime juice, chile powder, Worcestershire sauce and salt, then whisk in the oil. Marinate the birds, refrigerated, for 1 hour. Wrap the birds in a piece of bacon and secure with a toothpick.

Prepare medium-hot coals and grill the birds on both sides until they are just cooked through. Serve them with Mexican-style rice and/or steamed squash.

Serves 4.

Fried Doves or Quail

8 cleaned and plucked doves or quail
2 cups milk
1 1/2 teaspoons chile powder
1 teaspoon salt
2 cups flour
1/2 teaspoons salt
4 1/2 teaspoons chile powder
2 teaspoons garlic powder
Oil for deep frying (at least 3 cups)

Place the birds on a chopping block and flatten them with the palm of your hand or the back of a small iron skillet, then place them in a large bowl.

Mix together the milk, 1 1/2 teaspoons chile powder and salt, pour it over the birds and refrigerate for 1 hour. Mix together the flour, salt, 4-1/2 teaspoons chile powder and garlic powder in a shallow dish. Drain each bird and then dredge it in the flour mixture.

Refrigerate for 15 minutes, then again dip the birds in the milk mixture, coat with flour and refrigerate for another 15 minutes. Meanwhile, heat the cooking oil in a deep fryer or pot to 350 degrees.

When the oil is hot, fry the birds until golden-brown and cooked through. Serve with Mexican rice and /or steamed squash.

Serves 4.

CABRITO
(Kid)

Cabrito means kid or baby goat in Spanish. This northern Mexican specialty is also extremely popular in Tex-Mex home-style cooking. *Cabrito* is prepared either *al pastor* (cooked whole on a spit over mesquite coals) or *al horno* (in the oven), where it is usually cut into pieces and baked. *Cabrito* is not included on many restaurant menus because obtaining a ready supply of economically-priced kid in the United States, even in South Texas, is difficult.

In Mexico, *cabrito* usually refers to a baby goat that has not yet been weaned, which means it is less than around 30 days old. Older animals simply lack the tenderness and mild flavor necessary to produce an authentic *cabrito* dish. In northern Mexico, raising goats, especially dairy goats, is a big enterprise. Thus there is a large supply of kid, especially young males, that are considered surplus by dairy operations. That is not the case in Texas and most parts of the United States, where many goats, especially Angoras, are raised for their coats. The upshot is that, while plenty of older goats are available, there are few kids, especially at an affordable price. Home cooks usually either obtain a kid directly from a friend who raises them, or smuggle one in from Mexico.

Restaurants that do offer *cabrito* often use older animals. They either charbroil them, then wrap them in foil and bake in an oven until reasonably tender, or use the oven from the beginning. If done properly, these methods can produce a fairly tender result, but one with a flavor that is less mild than a true *cabrito* and with the inevitable boiled texture.

Bearing the above in mind, if you wish to make a home-style version of *cabrito al pastor* try the following recipe, which uses either a water smoker or kettle-style barbecue with the indirect heat method—coals placed at the edges of the grill and a pan of water in the center.

Mock Cabrito al Pastor

3 pounds leg of goat, cut into 6- to-8 inch pieces
1/2 cup lime juice
1/2 tablespoon salt
1 tablespoon chile powder
1/2 cup olive oil
Preheat an oven to 275 degrees.

Place soaked mesquite chips in a water smoker according the manufacturer's directions, or prepare an indirect fire in a kettle-style barbecue. Mix together the lime juice, salt and chile powder, then stir in the olive oil. Roast the meat until it reaches an internal temperature of 160 degrees, basting often with the oil/lime-juice mixture.

You can serve the cabrito at this time or wrap each piece of meat in aluminum foil and place in the preheated oven for 1 hour, which will yield a more tender result. Serve the *cabrito* with guacamole, hot tortillas, salsa and little bowls of *frijoles*.

Serves 4.

3
DESSERTS
FLAN TO
BUÑUELOS

DESSERTS:
FLAN TO BUÑUELOS

The truth is that desserts in Tex-Mex restaurants are not in much demand. Part of the reason is that by the time diners have finished several heaping baskets of chips served with multiple bowls of salsa, then put away something like a combination plate or platter of fajitas, there is not much room left.

Another reason is that this branch of Mexican cooking just does not have many truly interesting *postres* (desserts). This is notwithstanding the fact that Mexico's interior offers a cornucopia of sweets. Usually, if Tex-Mex eateries offer anything authentic it is a gelatinous flan or something with sales appeal—and nothing to do with Tex-Mex—such as "fried" ice cream.

FLAN

Probably the number one dessert served is the aforementioned flan. In most cases nobody but the most confirmed sweetaholic orders it, because it is usually so badly made. But that does not have to be the case, as the following recipe will demonstrate.

Traditional flan is made with eggs, milk or cream and sugar, and is baked with a caramel sauce. The following version takes it one step further by adding chocolate (which was originally from Mexico) and produces a dessert worthy of a five-star restaurant.

Chocolate Flan

3/4 cup sugar
1/4 cup water
3 tablespoons finely chopped pecans
4 eggs
1/4 cup cocoa powder (Valhrona is an excellent choice)
2 396-gram cans sweetened, condensed milk
10 ounces evaporated milk; this usually comes in 12 ounce
    (by volume) cans, so pour it into either a liquid measure
    or into an empty condensed milk can that is the right size
6 to 8 5-ounce, oven-proof ramekin dishes

Preheat your oven to 375 degrees. Place the sugar in a small skillet over medium heat until it has just melted. Slowly and carefully stir in the water and continue cooking, stirring as little as possible, until the mixture has turned a rich golden-brown. Pour the melted sugar into the ramekin dishes, making certain the entire bottoms are coated with the syrup.

Immediately sprinkle the nuts over the hot syrup, and allow the sugar to cool for a few minutes. Place the remaining ingredients in a blender, process for 2 minutes, then pour the contents into the ramekins, up to about 1/2 inch below the rims. Cut 6 to 8 pieces of tinfoil to fit over the top of the ramekins, and wrap them over the dishes to seal them. Place the dishes in a large casserole or oven-proof skillet and add very hot water until it reaches about half way up the dishes.

Put the whole affair into the oven. Bake the flan for 40 minutes, remove the casserole from the oven and the ramekins from the hot water, and allow them to cool for about 1 hour, then refrigerate them overnight.

To unmold the flan, put the bottom of the ramekins in warm water for about 20 to 30 seconds, run a sharp, thin knife around the edge of the flan to loosen it, then invert it onto a plate.

Serves 6 to 8.

BUÑUELOS

Buñuelos are a cross between a fritter and Indian fry bread and are popular throughout Mexico. They are especially esteemed in South Texas. San Antonio has several factories that turn out countless numbers of the crispy fried morsels for various celebrations.

They are made with a dough similar to the one for flour tortillas and shaped the same way, except thinner. But instead of being cooked on an ungreased griddle, they are fried in about 1/2 an inch of hot oil. *Buñuelos* are usually rolled into circles about 7 inches in diameter. However, at that size they are awkward and messy to eat, so I suggest you make what I call *buñuelitos*, a smaller version about 5 inches across. Because of the magic of geometry, they will have about half the surface area and be easier to handle.

After being fried, *buñuelos* are drizzled with a syrup flavored with anise, cinnamon and sometimes orange peel. They are then dusted with a mixture of cinnamon and sugar. The syrup is traditionally made with raw sugar piloncillo, which comes in solid cones. Either turbinado or brown sugar makes an excellent substitute. *Buñuelos* are usually eaten by themselves, but are also great to serve with other sweets, particularly ice cream.

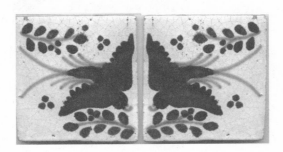

Buñuelos

The dough:
1 1/2 cups all-purpose flour
1/2 teaspoon baking powder
1/4 teaspoon salt
2 tablespoons melted butter
1 egg, beaten
2 tablespoons to 1/4 cup water

Whisk together the dry ingredients in a mixing bowl. Add and stir in the melted butter, then add and stir in the beaten egg. Using your fingers, mix the dough into a crumbly consistency like pie dough. Then add the water, 1 tablespoon at a time, until it comes together.

Work the dough for about 1 minute or until it is smooth and elastic. Cover the dough and allow it to rest for 1/2 hour.

The syrup:
1 cup turbinado, or light or dark brown sugar
1 cup water
1/2 teaspoon aniseed
Heaping 1/4 teaspoon cinnamon
Grated peel from 1 orange (outside, orange part only)

Stir all the ingredients together in a saucepan, bring to a boil, simmer for 2 minutes, then remove from the heat and reserve.

The sugar topping:
3 tablespoons sugar
1-1/2 teaspoons cinnamon
Mix the sugar and cinnamon together and reserve.

Making and serving the buñuelos

The reserved dough:
Vegetable oil
The reserved syrup
The reserved topping

To make traditionally-sized *buñuelos,* divide the dough into 3 balls of equal size, then divide each of them into 3 more balls for a total of 9.

To make *buñuelitos,* divide the dough into 6 balls of equal size, then divide each of them into 3 more balls for a total of 18.

Lightly flour a work surface and roll each ball into a circle of either 7 or 5 inches, depending on which option you chose. (Refer to the instructions for rolling flour tortillas.) Pour oil into a small skillet to a depth of about 1/2 an inch.

Heat the oil over medium heat just until a drop of water added to the oil instantly vaporizes. Be careful not to test the oil with more than 1 tiny drop of water at a time, as more can cause the oil to splatter and cause burns; if the oil begins to smoke it is way too hot. Carefully place a circle of flattened dough in the oil and cook until it is a light golden brown on the bottom, about 15 to 30 seconds. Turn the *buñuelo* and fry until the other side is also a light golden-brown. Remove the *buñuelo* to drain on absorbent towels, then fry the remaining dough in the same manner.

To serve, drizzle some of the reserved syrup onto each *buñuelo,* then dust with the flavored sugar.

Makes 9 buñuelos or 18 buñuelitos.

CAPIROTADA
(Bread Pudding)

*C*apirotada is much too good and too easy to prepare to serve only during during Lent, when it is traditionally made in Mexico. Knowing this, Tex-Mex cooks serve it year round.

Capirotada

The syrup:
6 ounces turbinado or light-brown sugar, just over 3/4 cup
1 1/3 cups water
1/4 teaspoon cinnamon
1/8 teaspoon powdered cloves
1/8 teaspoon allspice
2 tablespoons dark rum

Place all the ingredients in a saucepan, bring to a boil and simmer for 1 minute, then allow to cool and reserve.

The pudding:
12 slices French or firm-bodied sourdough bread
1/4 cup melted butter
3/4 cup grated Monterey Jack cheese
3/4 cup raisins
1/2 cup blanched, slivered almonds
A deep, 3-qt. casserole dish
The reserved syrup:
1/2 cup sour cream

Preheat your oven to 350 degrees. Place the bread on a baking sheet and toast it in the oven until it begins to harden on the top, but do not allow it to brown, about 3 1/2 minutes. Turn the bread over and continue baking it until the other side begins to harden, about another 3 minutes, again without browning.

Allow the bread to cool, then stack it, cut it into 4 pieces and place them in a large bowl. Toss the bread with the butter, cheese, raisins and almonds, then add all except 1/2 a cup of the syrup, and the sour cream. Toss the mixture vigorously until it is combined well and evenly. Pack the ingredients firmly into the casserole dish, pour the remaining 1/2 cup of the syrup over it, spread the sour cream on top, cover the dish, and place it in the oven.

Bake, covered, for 30 minutes.

Makes 6 to 8 servings.

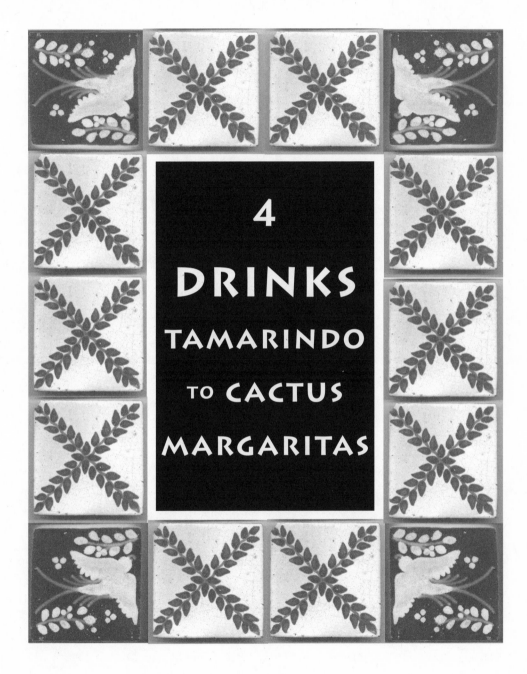

4

DRINKS

TAMARINDO

TO CACTUS

MARGARITAS

DRINKS:
TAMARINDO TO CACTUS MARGARITAS

Based on their popularity in restaurants, the drinks most associated with Tex-Mex food are margaritas, beer and cola. "This is just not a wine drinkin' food," said a friend, who added, "unless maybe you find one made last month with lots of bubbles." It is true that this earthy, nearly addictive cuisine tends to drown out any subtlety in beverages, but there is a drink category that is gaining in popularity that deserves mention.

In Mexico there is an entire class of drinks referred to as *aguas frescas,* or "fresh waters," that are made mostly with fruits and sugar: a version of soft drinks. Two of these, one made with tamarind and the other with hibiscus flowers, are becoming ever more popular in Texas barrios, and are even breaking into the mainstream. Called *tamarindo* and *jamaica,* their recipes will follow the one for the margarita.

MARGARITAS

Often recipes for the margarita begin with a discussion of the legends regarding who invented the first one. After participating in this fun myself, I have decided that we will never know for sure, and that I really don't care.

There are undoubtedly even more recipes than legends for this famous cocktail. Mixologists go on and on about whether to use silver, *reposado* or *añejo* tequila for the main ingredient, and whether to use triple sec, Grand Marnier or curaçao for the orange flavored liqueur. Almost everyone agrees that fresh lime juice is the only choice, but many contend that Key limes are a much better choice than Persian limes, and I agree with them.

Many restaurants offer all these permutations in endless combinations, from the ordinary bar margarita (often padded with limeade or one of those disgusting, artificially-colored margarita mixes) to super premium versions with ever-ascending prices.

ALL-PURPOSE MARGARITA

The recipe that comes most often to mind is the one that uses equal measures of silver tequila, triple sec and lime juice, not because it is necessarily the best, but because it is very good and easy to remember. You can make it "on the rocks" by shaking the ingredients with ice in a cocktail shaker and straining them over ice, or "up" by straining the shaken cocktail into a Margarita glass, or you can blend the ingredients with ice to make a frozen Margarita.

I suggest you start with one of those, using anything from a jigger to a quart measure, then vary the ingredients until you find your own Margarita nirvana. There are enough possible combinations so that the exercise may take a very long time.

CACTUS MARGARITAS

Cactus or prickly pear Margaritas are made from the tuna, or fruit of the nopal cactus. They are fast becoming Mexican restaurant favorites. The flavor of the extracted cactus fruit goes particularly well with tequila, and adds an extra dimension to this all-time favorite Mexican food accompaniment. In the southwest, supermarkets often stock tunas that have been trimmed of their small but very sharp spines, as do Hispanic groceries in other parts of the country.

Since tunas are full of tiny seeds, a juice extractor that automatically removes them is the first choice. The tuna can also be chopped up and blended with the other ingredients, but the results must be carefully strained.

Cactus Margaritas

    4 tunas or cactus fruits
    4 shots silver tequila
    4 shots lime juice
    4 shots triple sec

Put the tunas through a juice extractor, which should yield about 1 cup juice. Place the extracted juice and remaining ingredients in a blender. If you wish to make frozen Margaritas, add a couple of handfuls of ice and blend, or blend without the ice and pour over rocks.

Makes 4 drinks.

EXOTIC FRUIT MARGARITAS

These are made the same way as Cactus Margaritas, except that the juice is more readily available, fresh, frozen or canned. Use any juice you fancy: mango, guava and pineapple are popular choices. You can also add some fresh strawberries to the blender. If you do not like your drinks too sweet you can reduce the amount of triple sec to 2 shots.

Exotic Fruit Margaritas

    1 cup exotic fruit juice
    4 shots silver tequila
    4 shots lime juice
    4 shots triple sec

Place the juice and remaining ingredients in a blender. If you wish to make frozen Margaritas, add a couple handfuls of ice and blend, or blend without ice and pour over rocks.

Makes 4 drinks.

MEXICAN MOJITO

This drink adapts the famous Cuban rum drink to Mexico's national beverage to make a refreshing summer cocktail.

Mexican Mojito

1 shot white tequila
1 1/2 teaspoons lime juice
1 teaspoon sugar
6 mint leaves
Club soda

Place all ingredients except the soda into a cocktail shaker and stir vigorously, crushing the mint leaves a little in the process. Pour the mixed ingredients into a tall glass over ice, add soda to fill and stir just until mixed.

Makes 1 drink.

JAMAICA
(Hibiscus Soft Drink)

*J*amaica is a lovely red-colored tea made from dried hibiscus flowers. While it is sometimes taken hot, it is usually made into a refreshing soft drink by adding sugar to the tea, and sometimes a squeeze of lime juice, and serving it over ice.

Jamaica

4 cups water
1 1/2 tablespoons *jamaica* (dried hibiscus leaves, either sold
    in bulk or tea bags)
1/2 cup sugar
2 tablespoons lime juice
6 mint leaves

Bring water to a boil, pour over the *jamaica* and allow to steep, covered, for 15 minutes. Strain out and discard *jamaica*. Stir sugar into liquid, bring to a boil, turn off the heat, add the mint leaves, and allow to steep, uncovered, for 3 minutes. Remove mint leaves, allow to cool and serve iced.

You can also make a base by following the directions but using only 2 cups water, then topping the base with club soda in iced glasses.

Makes 1 quart.

TAMARINDO

Tamarindo is usually made like a tea by boiling the paste from tamarind pods in water, then adding sugar. You can certainly use the tamarind pots if you wish, but you will spend a lot of time removing the stringy filaments and seeds. Much better is to buy concentrated tamarind paste, which can be found at Asian groceries. But beware, as it comes in two forms: one is a paste that includes the seeds and has to be dissolved and strained. The best alternative is to buy the concentrate that contains no seeds.

Tamarindo

4 teaspoons tamarind concentrate, without seeds
1 quart water
1/2 cup sugar

Place all ingredients in a saucepan, bring to a boil, simmer for 1 minute, then allow to cool. Serve over ice.

Makes 1 quart.

5

TEXAS

BARBECUE

TEXAS BARBECUE

Let's be clear! To make the very best Texas barbecue—or any other style— at home requires an investment in both time and equipment. You do not just season the meat and put it into an oven for a set amount of time. The best barbecue is smoked using hardwood as the fuel, so just controlling the heat takes experience. Some of the factors involved include the type of wood, size of the wood used, how dry it is, how well the dampers on your pit regulate the heat and the outside temperature.

That's the bad news.

The good news is that if you really want to produce superlative barbecue, you will spend the time and money required. The really good news is that if you just want to make very good barbecue you will be able to do so with a minimum of practice, and at a very low cost.

Barbecue means different things in different parts of the United States. To many it simply relates to grilling over wood or charcoal. To people in the South, barbecue involves cooking pork or an entire pig on a rotisserie over direct heat, or in a pit with indirect heat. To people in the lower Midwest, especially Kansas, it means cooking ribs over indirect heat, often on huge enclosed rotisseries. In parts of the Northwest and Alaska, barbecue is often translated into the ancient Indian technique of smoking salmon in pits or roasting it on cedar planks. In Hawaii, barbecuing involves smoking a pig wrapped in banana leaves, burying it in a pit and then dousing it with salted water.

Texas-style barbecue includes the ribs, sausage and chicken found in other parts of the country, but what really sets it apart is its traditional beef brisket. Texans take immeasurable pride in turning this tough, ungainly cut of meat into a mouth-wateringly tender delicacy.

Most Texas barbecue is smoked in a pit with indirect heat, but in West Texas direct heat is used as well. There are also regional differences regarding the fuel. While the heat source of choice in various parts of the country includes hickory, pecan, apple wood, alder and others, in Texas it is almost always either oak or mesquite, or a combination of both.

As with all stereotypes there are exceptions, and that is true for the above descriptions. Yes, you can find pork, goat and even armadillo barbecued in Texas, and some cooks use pecan and other woods or even charcoal in place of oak or mesquite. But for our purposes it is indeed the mesquite, oak, and beef brisket that most sets Texas barbecue apart from the other styles.

The principal method of cooking brisket involves coating the meat with a spice rub, then, as the meat smokes, mopping it with a spicy sauce called a "mop", which rarely contains tomato or much sugar because both will burn, creating a bitter flavor.

Texas barbecue is actually a combination or fusion of traditions from the South, native Indians and early German settlers. The original pit was basically a hole in the ground in which wood was burned to coals so the meat could be cooked on grills above them. Since then barbecue has been cooked in everything from converted refrigerators and commercial baking ovens to cannibalized trash cans, with and without rotisserie implements.

Most Texas barbecue can now be separated into two styles, based on the equipment used: one where the meat is cooked with smoke and indirect heat, and the other where it is cooked directly over coals, albeit at a considerable distance from them.

Probably the majority of Texas barbecue is made in a special smoker first introduced by German meat markets. They built huge, brick pits with offset fireboxes that permit only smoke and heat to touch the meat. The construction of these pits is now often echoed in portable pits that look like a giant horizontal iron pipe on legs with an offset firebox in which logs smolder at one end and with a vertical chimney at the other. In fact, early models were made from used oil-field pipe and barrels. The draft from the chimney draws the smoke and heat across the meat so that it is never touched by flame or direct heat.

In West Texas, and sometimes in other areas, coals are prepared in a separate firebox and shoveled into the bottom of rectangular pits of steel or brick. The meat is placed on grills 2 1/2 to 3 feet above the coals and turned from time to time as it cooks. This closely imitates the early earthen pits.

Like most other smoke-cooking traditions, Texas barbecue is usually cooked at a temperature of between 200 and 250 degrees, though some pit masters use higher heat during part of the process. To obtain the desired result, which is a brisket that is crispy brown on the outside and very tender with a red inside ring from the smoke on the inside, this usually translates into a cooking time of between 1 and 1 1/2 hours per pound.

BARBECUE BRISKET

Preparing contest-winning brisket at home requires considerable dedication. In order to obtain a perfectly-smoked result that will impress even the most jaded purist, you must have the proper equipment, the proper cut of meat, the proper fuel, lots of experience, and be willing to spend 9 to 18 hours watching temperatures, tending coals, and mopping the meat. All this for a process that can basically be summed up by saying that you smoke the meat at between 200 to 250 degrees until it is very tender!

If you simply follow this rule you may not receive kudos from hard-core barbecue aficionados, but you will delight yourself and your guests.

In terms of equipment, the pros and serious amateurs usually use a Texas-style smoker such as the one described above, several models of which are now distributed throughout the country or can be ordered. Authentic barbecue brisket is made with the entire piece, called the "market cut." These usually weigh between 9 and 13 pounds and include a large amount of fat on the top, which is responsible for the otherwise tough cut's eventual tenderness. Unfortunately this cut can be difficult or impossible to find outside of Texas, where most brisket is cut into smaller pieces and well-trimmed.

As noted above, properly smoking a brisket can take 9 to 18 hours. Because of the long cooking time, most traditional pit masters cook their briskets during the night and stop serving when the meat is gone in the early to mid afternoon. If any brisket is left over, some wrap it in foil and reheat it the next day.

In the process of doing this, cooks discovered that an even more tender result is possible. Playing off this discovery, some pit masters now cook their brisket for a much shorter period of time, wrap it in foil and finish it off with a couple of hours of additional smoking. Some take the process further and do the final cooking in an oven, where the heat is much easier to regulate.

As might be imagined, there is considerable dispute over the foil-oven method. Purists maintain that unless they see the reddish imprint of smoke throughout the meat, indicating that the process was done entirely with smoke, the barbecue is not authentic. Others enjoy the softer, more tender texture of brisket that has been wrapped in foil. Some cooks, particularly in East Texas, take the process even further, creating a result that is as falling-apart tender as Southern Style pulled pork. To me, this is entirely a matter of personal taste.

Recommended equipment:

First, I do not recommend the West Texas, direct-heat style of barbecue to people for whom barbecuing is not a real passion. The pit itself is not universally available for purchase, which means a fair amount of construction. And preparing the coals in a separate fire box and getting them into the pit is simply more trouble than most people want to go to.

For purists, the traditional Texas-style apparatus with an offset firebox is the best option. The disadvantages are that these are very heavy and difficult to move, take up a fair amount of space and range in price from about $350 to more than $1,500 for a top-quality home size model. Also, during the long cooking process the temperature must be constantly checked and the fire adjusted accordingly.

While decent brisket can be made in a kettle-style barbecue, where the indirect heat process is achieved by placing the coals on two sides with a pan of water in between, I do not recommend it. This method requires temperature checks as frequent as with a traditional smoker and replacing coals as often as the West Texas method. The results are usually not as good, as it is easy for the temperature to climb too high and scorch and dry the meat.

However, for the occasional smoke cook who does not want to invest in additional equipment, use of a kettle-style barbecue is a viable option, especially if you have a model with a hinged grill to facilitate adding additional coals. But be sure and use an oven thermometer to ensure you are cooking close to the desired temperature.

For the cook who wants to make good Texas-style barbecue infrequently and do so with a minimum of trouble, I recommend the same piece of equipment as for Mexican *barbacoa*—a water smoker. These devices produce decent smoke flavor and a tender result in about the same amount of time as a traditional smoker, with far less effort.

You can use a gas or charcoal water smoker, but I prefer the ones powered by electricity. Because devices for measuring the remaining amount of propane are imperfect, gas models can run out of fuel in the middle of the process. Charcoal smokers require several additions of glowing briquettes during cooking, which can mean removing the hot brisket and its grill and the even hotter water dish. After plugging it in, all the electric model needs is the addition of water and wood chips about every 2 to 3 hours. Water can be poured through the top, and additional soaked wood chips can usually be placed with ease through a small door on the smoker's side.

In terms of fuel, I recommend a combination of oak and mesquite chips. While I love the flavor of mesquite, it will give a bitter, off taste to the meat if used during the entire cooking time. Therefore, with an electric smoker, I use mesquite chips soaked in water during the first two hours of cooking, then switch to oak chips. The only problem is that in many parts of the country they are not available. In that case use hickory chips, which are distributed nationwide.

When using a water smoker you can use the foil method, which means wrapping the meat in foil after about 5 hours, or when the temperature reaches 165 to 170 degrees, and continuing to cook it either in the smoker or in an oven at 250 degrees for an additional hour, or until the temperature reaches 185 degrees. However, it is easy for the meat to over-steam, giving it the texture and much of the taste of baked or braised brisket.

Instead, I suggest you continue smoking the meat until the desired tenderness is reached. The exact time depends on the size of the meat, the internal temperature of the smoker and the outside temperature. These variables can change the cooking time by an hour or more.

The best approach is to persevere and continue smoking until the meat is very tender. For a 10-pound brisket this will usually be 9 to 10 hours. After about 5 hours the meat will usually be between 160 and 170 degrees and will have a great flavor, but will still be quite tough. At some point, usually around 9 hours or a little more, you will find the meat temperature nearing 185 degrees and discover that it has suddenly become amazingly tender, so just keep going and have faith!

While the following directions pertain specifically to the electric water smoker, good brisket can be prepared using many other devices. Simply bear in mind the principle mentioned earlier: smoke the meat at between 200 and 250 degrees until it is very tender.

Barbecued Electric-Water-Smoker Beef Brisket

The rub:
2 tablespoons pure chile powder, preferably from *ancho* chiles
2 1/2 tablespoons salt
2 tablespoons dark brown sugar
1 teaspoon dry mustard
1 tablespoon dried, granulated garlic
1 1/2 teaspoons dried, granulated onion
1 tablespoon black pepper
3 tablespoons sweet paprika

Mix all the ingredients together and reserve.

The mop:
2 tablespoons brown sugar
3/4 cup vegetable oil
1/4 cup butter
1/3 cup white vinegar
2 tablespoons fresh lime juice
1 head garlic, cloves separated but not peeled
1 medium onion, peeled and quartered
1 12-ounce bottle beer
1 tablespoon oregano
4 teaspoons Worcestershire sauce
4 teaspoons soy sauce

Place all the ingredients in a large saucepan, bring to a boil, then simmer, stirring to make sure all the sugar is dissolved, for 10 minutes. Reserve.

Preparing the brisket:

1 market-cut brisket, about 10 to 11 pounds

Hardwood smoking chips such as mesquite, oak, pecan or hickory

The reserved rub

The reserved mop

The night before you prepare the brisket, coat it with the rub on all sides and refrigerate it. In this case the name rub is accurate, because the spices need to be vigorously massaged into the meat.

Remove the meat from the refrigerator about 2 to 3 hours before you begin to smoke in order to bring up the temperature. About 20 minutes before smoking, put about 3 handfuls of hardwood chips in a bowl and cover it with water.

Just before plugging in your electric water smoker, discard the soaking water and place the chips near the heating element per the manufacturer's recommendations. Fill the water pan with boiling water, install the grill, place the meat on it, put the top on the grill and plug it in.

After 2 hours, carefully pour additional boiling water into the pan and replace the cover on the smoker. After a total of 4 hours, add additional soaked chips and more water to the pan and continue smoking. After a total of 6 hours, add more water. After a total of 8 hours, add more smoking chips and water and continue smoking until the meat is quite tender, which will be when it reaches a temperature of about 185 degrees.

Remove the meat from the smoker and place it on a chopping block. Using a large carving knife, slice off as much of the fat from the top of the brisket as possible, then slice it sideways—against the grain—into slices less than 1/4-inch thick.

BARBECUED RIBS

Even in beef-conscious Texas, barbecued ribs usually refer to pork spareribs, although some barbecue places also serve beef and lamb ribs. The difference between barbecued ribs usually relates to how they are seasoned and to how tender they are.

In terms of flavor, for the following recipe you can use the rub and mop for brisket, adding a little more brown sugar to the rub for sweetness, or you can try the orange juice and *ancho* chile marinade that follows. It is similar to the one used by street vendors to make the meat for the tacos *al pastor* one sees so often roasting on vertical spits in Mexico.

When it comes to texture, I must confess my preference is for ribs that are so tender they nearly fall off the bone. If you agree with that, follow the directions for finishing the ribs in an oven after 4 hours of smoking. If you like them a little chewier, simply leave them in the smoker for another hour or two.

As with the brisket recipe, the specific instructions are designed for an electric water smoker. If you plan to use other equipment, try to keep them smoking at between 225 to 250 degrees for the specified times.

Barbecued Ribs

Seasoning the ribs:
For about 6 pounds pork spare ribs

Alternative 1—Using a rub
Add 2 tablespoons brown sugar to the brisket rub recipe and massage it into the ribs the night before you smoke them.

Alternative 2—Using a Mexican-style marinade
2 medium-sized *ancho* chiles, stems and seeds removed
3 cloves garlic, peeled and coarsely chopped

1 teaspoon salt
1 teaspoon black pepper
1/2 tablespoon dried, leaf oregano
3/4 cup orange juice

Tear the chiles into small pieces and place them in a blender, add remaining ingredients and allow the chiles to re-hydrate for about 15 minutes. Blend the ingredients for 2 minutes at high speed. Pour the blended marinade over the ribs and leave them in your refrigerator overnight.

Smoking the ribs:

Remove the ribs from the refrigerator about 1 1/2 hours before you begin to smoke them. Soak and add hardwood smoking chips to a water smoker, according to the manufacturer's directions.

When you are ready to begin smoking, fill the water dish with boiling water, place the ribs on the grill above it, place the top on the grill and plug in the smoker. Baste the ribs with the brisket mop or, if you use the marinade, with excess marinade for 4 hours. Add water to the water pan about every 2 hours.

At this point you can either continue smoking the ribs until they are adequately tender—about 5 to 6 hours total—or you can finish them in the oven, which will make them extremely tender. To do this, place the ribs in a foil baking dish after they have smoked for 4 hours. Cover the dish tightly with foil and place it in an oven preheated to 325 degrees for 1 1/2 hours.

Remove the covered foil pan from the oven and place it inside a brown paper grocery bag (a good reason for requesting paper rather than plastic), fold to seal at the end or slip another bag over the package if the baking dish is too large, and let it rest for 45 minutes. Open the foil dish just before serving and you will have some of the most tender ribs you have ever tasted!

SAUSAGE

The German influence on Texas barbecue ensured that sausage is a prominent component. You can barbecue any type of sausage, but the Polish-style ones are most popular.

While tough meats such as brisket and ribs need long cooking to make them tender, that is not the case with sausage, which is made with ground meat. In fact, the juiciest sausage is one that has been just cooked through; overcooking will make it dry and leathery. An hour or two in the smoker, depending on the size and amount of sausage and how you like them done, is usually ample. Simply add your sausage about an hour before whatever else you are smoking will be done. It s that simple!

BARBECUE SAUCE

There are countless barbecue sauces, as a quick perusal of grocery shelves will confirm. The sauces served at most Texas barbecue joints are just as varied but the majority use a catsup base, with additions of vinegar, sugar and chile peppers in one way or another. Some also add drippings from the meat.

This one is a favorite of mine, as it is both easy to make and gets its smoky touch from naturally smoked chipotle chile peppers rather than from liquid smoke.

Barbecue Sauce

1 cup Heinz catsup
1 cup water
2 to 3 (or more to taste) canned *chipotle* chile peppers,
    minced
2 tablespoons cider vinegar
2 tablespoons white vinegar
1 tablespoon brown sugar

Stir all ingredients together in a saucepan, bring to a boil and simmer for 2 minutes. Reserve or refrigerate until ready to use.

Makes a little over 2 cups of sauce.

POTATO SALAD

Many people like to prepare dishes such as potato salad and coleslaw by throwing all the ingredients together and measuring by feel. Therefore, I offer the following recipe as a guide or beginning point. It is excellent as is, but will be even better when modified to your own personal taste.

Potato Salad

2 1/2 pounds white or red boiling potatoes, peeled and cut
    into 1/2-inch pieces
1 teaspoon salt for the cooking water
1/4 cup Mexican style *chorizo,* casing removed
3 tablespoons mayonnaise
1 1/2 teaspoons American, yellow mustard
2 teaspoons sweet pickle relish
1 teaspoon freshly ground black pepper
1/2 teaspoon sweet paprika
2 green onions, minced
2 tablespoons minced parsley
1/2 teaspoon salt or to taste

Place the potatoes in a saucepan, cover them with water by 1 inch, stir in the 1 teaspoon salt, bring to a boil and then simmer until the potatoes are just tender. Strain off and discard the water, cover the potatoes with cold water and add about 1 cup of ice cubes to cool them quickly. When the potatoes are properly chilled, drain off the water, dry and reserve them.

Heat a small skillet over medium heat, add the *chorizo* and cook, chopping the *chorizo* into tiny pieces with the side of a spoon until it is golden-brown. Pour the *chorizo* and any grease from the pan into the potatoes and toss. In a small bowl, mix together the remaining ingredients. Add the resulting dressing to the potatoes and *chorizo*. Toss until thoroughly combined.

Serves 4.

COLESLAW

Coleslaw consists of shredded cabbage and other vegetables mixed with a dressing that is either creamy with a mayonnaise or cream base, or made with vinegar and oil. There is no traditional Texas coleslaw, so use your favorite recipe or try one of the following two representing outstanding versions of each dressing.

Uncooked cabbage is very crisp but also tough, and has a bitter taste. Cooked cabbage lacks the bitterness but is too limp for coleslaw. To solve this problem, pour a little boiling water over the shredded cabbage, then immerse it in cold water to immediately stop the cooking process. The result will be tender without bitterness, yet still crispy.

A good way to do this is to wash the shredded cabbage in the basket of a salad spinner, pour a cup or two of boiling water over it, then put it under a faucet of cold water. When the cabbage has cooled, spin it dry.

Spicy, Creamy Coleslaw

The following recipe was adapted from one presented on Martha Stewart's Food Channel program, and is terrific.

The slaw:
1 1/2 pounds shredded green cabbage (or a mixture of green
     and purple cabbage) (approximately 12 cups)
1/2 large white onion, thinly sliced
1/2 bell pepper, thinly sliced
1/2 large carrot, shredded
3/4 cup peeled jícama, sliced into julienne strips

Wash the cabbage in a strainer, pour 1 1/2 cups boiling water over it, then cool it under a faucet of cold water. Dry the cooled cabbage, mix it with the remaining ingredients and reserve.

The dressing:
3 tablespoons cider vinegar
3 tablespoons yellow mustard
2 tablespoons Heinz catsup
2 tablespoons sour cream
1 tablespoon mayonnaise
3/4 teaspoon salt
1/2 teaspoon Tabasco sauce
1/4 teaspoon Worcestershire sauce
1/4 cup sugar

Place all the ingredients except the sugar is a saucepan and bring to a boil. Put the reserved slaw in a bowl and pour the hot dressing over it. Immediately sprinkle the sugar over the slaw and toss thoroughly. Refrigerate the slaw until very cold, about 2 hours.

Serves 4

Mexican-Style Coleslaw

This is a vinegar and oil style coleslaw similar to those often served with Mexican combination plates in California and Arizona.

The slaw:
1 1/2 pounds shredded green cabbage (or a mixture of green and purple cabbage) (approximately 12 cups)
4 green onions, minced
1 *poblano* chile, thinly sliced

Wash the cabbage in a strainer, mix in the other ingredients and pour 2 cups of boiling water over it. Immediately cool it off under a faucet of cold water, then dry and reserve it in a large bowl.

The dressing:
1 1/2 tablespoons cider vinegar
1 1/2 tablespoons malt vinegar
1 1/2 tablespoons water
2 1/4 teaspoons salt
1 teaspoon black pepper
1 teaspoon sugar
1 1/2 teaspoons Dijon mustard
3 tablespoons olive oil

Whisk together all ingredients except the olive oil, then whisk in the oil in a steady stream. Toss the dressing with the slaw ingredients and refrigerate for at least 2 hours.

Serves 4

BEANS

The beans served with Texas barbecue are almost always pinto beans. Some cooks add chile powder to their beans, but most aficionados are scornful of this practice, and sugar is never added. To my taste, the *frijoles de olla* found in the Tex-Mex section are the perfect barbecue accompaniment.

6

TEXAS CHILE

TEXAS CHILE

Chile is a dish about which there is a great deal of affection—and disagreement. Some of the disputed issues include whether to use meat that is chopped into small pieces, finely ground or a coarse chile-grind, whether to include beans, what kind of chiles to use, whether to use chile powder or whole chiles, whether to include tomatoes, whether to use pork, venison, goat and other meats besides beef, and whether to garnish the chile with cheese and/or raw onions.

Fortunately, most of the controversy falls into the category of good fun. Other than in the politics of chile contests, where arguments can become heated (pun intended), the subject is one of the few things about which people can disagree without becoming angry.

Most evidence indicates that chile became popular in Texas on ranches and during cattle drives, where beef and chiles were made into a delicious, nourishing stew that was a reward for a hard day's work. Over the years, as the subject caught the nation's imagination, regional versions developed as did fanciful variations, invented to catch the eyes and palettes of judges in chile contests.

The subject of chile has been well covered in books and magazine articles, with the definitive work still being *A Bowl of Red* by Francis X. Tolbert, who chronicled the dish's history and early permutations. Included in the latter is "son-of-a-bitch stew," which adds *tripa de leche,* the tube that connects the cow's two stomachs, brains, sweetbreads, tongue and heart to the more common ingredients. With the recent regulations related to mad cow disease, many of these ingredients will no longer be readily available.

There is a significant difference between Texas and Tex-Mex chiles, primarily regarding the quantity of beef and chiles. Tex-Mex chile stews were developed by those forced to make do with limited resources. The result is a stew with less meat and fewer spices, which creates a more subtle result. *Carne guisada* (see recipe index) is a good example. Texas chiles, on the other hand, are bold, beefy, in-your-face hot dishes.

Like most Texans, I think my version of chile—an adaptation of Tolbert's— is the best. While I have attended chile contests and sampled some of the more complex and creative versions, it is the original, or something close to it, that keeps me coming back. This rendition has the power of a truly great comfort food that is unequaled on a cold winter's night.

As Tolbert says, "Real chile con carne is a haunting, mystic thing." Certainly you can add different chiles, spices and other flavorings—2 bay leaves and a tablespoon of vinegar are good ones—and the results may be delicious, but at some point you lose the genius of the original's simplicity. So it is my favorite version of this classic dish that is presented below.

TEXAS-STYLE CHILE

The following recipe departs from the original by adding a little tomato sauce for its touch of sweetness, the use of cooking oil rather than beef suet and the addition of a little paprika. I have tried—and you can use—almost any cut of beef, but to my taste the special flavor and texture of skirt steak is as good as it gets. You may cut the meat into 1/2-inch pieces or grind it coarsely in a food processor, as you wish, but I prefer the latter.

Although I have specified whole *ancho* chiles, which impart a smooth, well-rounded heat, you can substitute 1 tablespoon of powdered, pure *ancho* chile per whole chile pepper. However, the dish will not be nearly as smooth or as naturally thick. You can also substitute 1/4 teaspoon of cayenne pepper for each *de árbol* or *japones* chile pepper. I especially like this chile served garnished with grated mild cheddar cheese, and have included it. To be authentically minimal, simply leave out the tomato sauce and paprika.

The traditional way of serving chile is in a bowl with beans and hot tortillas on the side. However, I must confess that my favorite is to mound the chile on steamed rice and top it with the cheese.

Texas-Style Chile

6 *ancho* chiles, stems and seeds removed and torn into small
    pieces
4 *chiles de árbol* or *japones* chiles, stems and seeds removed
7 cloves peeled garlic
1/2 cup chopped onion
1 1/2 teaspoons oregano
1 1/2 teaspoons ground cumin
1 cup water
2 tablespoons cooking oil
2 pounds skirt steak or beef stew meat, either cut into 1/2-
    inch pieces or chile-grind
1 cup water
1 8-ounce can tomato sauce
2 teaspoons hot paprika
1 teaspoon salt, or to taste
2 tablespoons Masa Harina or Maseca, or substitute all-pur
    pose flour
Water
1 cup grated mild cheddar cheese

Place the *ancho* and *chiles de árbol* or *japones* chiles in a bowl, cover them with very hot tap water and allow them to soak for 20 minutes. Drain off and discard the water. Put the rehydrated chiles in a blender with the garlic, onion, oregano and cumin, add the first 1 cup water, blend for 2 minutes at high speed and reserve.

Heat a heavy pot or Dutch oven over medium-high to high heat, add 1 tablespoon of the oil, then brown 1 pound of the beef and remove it from the pot. Repeat the process with the remaining cooking oil and meat, then replace the previously browned meat. Add the second 1 cup water, the tomato sauce, paprika and the salt.

Bring the liquid to a simmer, cover the pot and cook at a low simmer for 1 3/4 hours or until the meat is very tender. Meanwhile mix the *masa* or flour with 2 tablespoons water and reserve.

When the meat is very tender, remove the top of the pot and stir in about one-half of the *masa* mix. Continue simmering the chile, uncovered, for about 10 minutes or until thickened, adding a little more of the *masa*-water mix, if necessary. Serve the chile garnished with the cheese.

Serves 4.

ACKNOWLEDGMENTS

After writing three books chronicling different aspects of Mexican cooking, I had always wanted to do one that included only the very best recipes, the ones I would recommend to restaurant clients. For allowing me to do that, and for their unstinting support, I thank Lewis and Mary Fisher of Maverick Publishing. I would also like to thank Colleen Daley for her attention to detail in the editing and to Barbara Whitehead for her terrific design. Thanks to Frances Chenburg and Roger Chenburg for proof reading, and for apt suggestions. Many thanks to Diana Barrios for the kind words.

I owe the greatest debt to my wife Andrea, not least for the illustrations and for innumerable washed dishes.

None of this, of course, would have been possible without the countless Tejano cooks who created and nurtured Tex-Mex cooking, so thanks to them, too.

INGREDIENT SOURCES

For Mexican ingredients I recommend Mex-Grocer.com., which can be reached on the Internet at www.mexgrocer.com.

Also reliable for high quality *ancho* chiles and chile powder is Penzey's Spices. They can be reached on the Internet at www.penzey's.com or by telephone at (800) 741-7787.

Acknowledgments

The cover illustration is *Chili Queens at the Alamo,* an undated oil painted by Julian Onderdonk (1882–1922) now in the collection of San Antonio's Witte Museum. Steam rises from a bowl of chile con carne, a favorite among the spicy evening foods served on open tables in the public plazas of San Antonio through the early twentieth century.

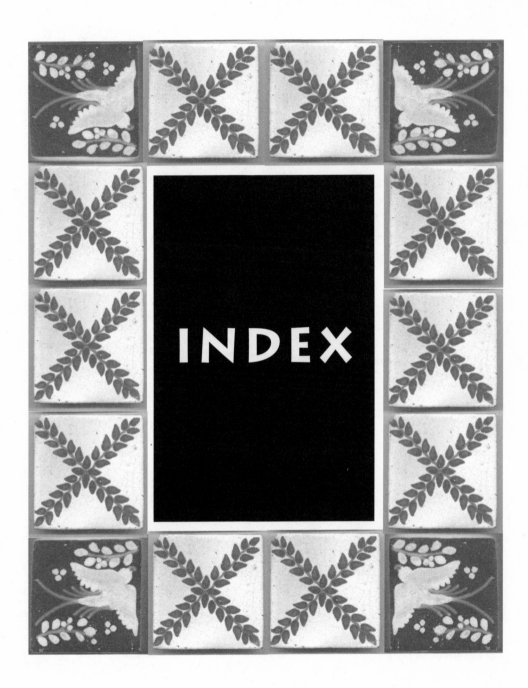

INDEX

INDEX